# TALLIS'S
# ILLUSTRATED SCRIPTURE HISTORY

FOR THE

## IMPROVEMENT OF YOUTH.

BY

THE EDITOR OF STURM'S FAMILY DEVOTIONS.

VOL. II.

PUBLISHED BY JOHN TALLIS AND COMPANY,
LONDON AND NEW YORK.

# INDEX.

## VOL II.

| | PAGE |
|---|---|
| Adultery, the Woman taken in | 201 |
| Ananias, the Death of | 243 |
| Apostles, Christ preparing the | 233 |
| Antioch, Paul at | 263 |
| Barren Fig-tree, Christ curses the | 79 |
| Bartimaeus, Christ restoring to Sight | 77 |
| Betrayed, Christ | 39 |
| Blind Man, Christ restores Sight to the | 71 |
| Bloody Issue, a woman cured of a | 155 |
| Brother, the Prodigal's | 167 |
| Cana, the Marriage at | 191 |
| Canaan, Christ and the Woman of | 25 |
| Charger, John the Baptist's Head brought in a | 67 |
| Children, Zebedee's | 29 |
| Christ, the Temptation of | 11 |
| ——— Peter denying | 41 |
| ——— Precious Ointment poured on the Head of | 89 |
| ——— the Ascension of | 111 |
| ——— Angels proclaim the Birth of | 123 |
| ——— Judas betrays | 175 |
| ——— scourged | 215 |
| ——— the Dead | 221 |
| Cleansed, the Leper | 61 |
| Comforter, Christ the | 139 |
| Commandments, the First to the Tenth | 285—304 |
| Cornelius, the Angel appearing to | 255 |
| Council, Christ led before the | 177 |
| Cross, Christ taken from the | 47 |
| ——— Simon the Cyrenian compelled to bear the | 99 |
| ——— Vinegar given to Christ on the | 101 |
| ——— Christ bearing the | 217 |
| ——— Christ on the | 219 |
| Crucified, Christ | 179 |
| Daughter, raising of Jairus's | 19 |
| Devils, Christ casts out a Legion of | 153 |

| | PAGE |
|---|---|
| Disciples, Christ appears to his | 109 |
| ——— Christ sends forth his | 157 |
| ——— Christ discourses with his | 171 |
| ——— Jesus going forth with his | 211 |
| ——— Mary Magdalene and the | 223 |
| Doctors, Christ disputing with the | 131 |
| Dragon, Michael and the | 283 |
| Dream, Joseph warned in a | 7 |
| Emmaus, Christ at | 185 |
| Ephesus, Paul preaching at | 273 |
| Eutychus, Paul restoring Life to | 275 |
| Eyes of the Blind, Jesus opening the | 31 |
| Family, the Holy | 129 |
| Father, the Prodigal Son leaves his | 161 |
| ——— the Prodigal Son returns to his | 165 |
| Feet, the Woman anointing Christ's | 149 |
| ——— Behold my Hands and my | 187 |
| ——— Christ washing the Disciples' | 209 |
| Felix, Paul before | 277 |
| Fishes, the Miraculous Draught of | 143 |
| ——— the Great Draught of | 229 |
| Garden, Christ's agony in the | 37 |
| Garment, a Woman touches the Hem of Christ's | 17 |
| Ghost, Descent of the Holy | 235 |
| God, the Lamb of | 189 |
| High Priest, Jesus taken before the | 93 |
| ——— Peter before the | 241 |
| Impotent Man, Christ curing the | 197 |
| Innocents, Murder of the | 9 |
| Jerusalem, Christ entering | 33 |
| ——— St. Peter's first Sermon in | 237 |
| Jesus, the Resurrection of | 51 |

# INDEX.

| | PAGE |
|---|---|
| Jesus, Simon and Andrew called by | 57 |
| —— Joseph of Aremathæa begs the body of | 103 |
| —— an Angel proclaims the Resurrection of | 105 |
| —— the Naming of | 127 |
| —— the Entombment of | 181 |
| —— Martha meets | 203 |
| —— Mary anointing the feet of | 207 |
| John, St., the Infant | 119 |
| ———— Preaching | 53 |
| ———— Baptizing | 55 |
| Judas, Repentance of | 43 |
| Lame Man, Peter and John curing the | 239 |
| Lazarus, Raising of | 205 |
| Little Children, Christ blessing | 75 |
| Lystra, Paul and Barnabas at | 265 |
| —— Paul stoned at | 267 |
| Magdalene, Christ appearing to Mary | 225 |
| Mary, Christ appearing to | 107 |
| —— an Angel appearing to the Virgin | 115 |
| —— Elizabeth visited by | 117 |
| Money-changers, Christ casting out the | 81 |
| —— the Tribute | 83 |
| Mite, the Widow's | 85 |
| Mount, Sermon on the | 13 |
| Multitude, Jesus feeds the | 69 |
| —— Christ feeding the | 199 |
| Nativity, the | 121 |
| Nobleman's Son, Christ curing the | 195 |
| Palsy, Christ healing one Sick of the | 63 |
| Peter, Christ's charge to | 231 |
| —— Cornelius meeting | 257 |
| Pharisees, Christ disputing with the | 73 |
| Philippi, Paul at | 269 |
| Pilate, Christ led forth by | 213 |
| Prophesy, they bade him | 95 |
| Prison, Peter delivered out of | 259 |
| Prison, Paul and Silas in | 271 |
| Publican, the Pharisee and the | 169 |
| Repentance, Peter's | 97 |
| Samaria, Christ and the Woman of | 193 |
| Samaritan, the Good | 159 |
| Sapphira, the Death of | 245 |
| Saul, Conversion of | 249 |
| Saviour, the | 1 |
| Sea, Christ walking on the | 23 |
| Sepulchre, the two Marys at the | 49 |
| ———— Women viewing the | 183 |
| Servant, Christ healing the Centurion's | 145 |
| Shepherds, Adoration of the | 125 |
| Ship, Christ teaching from the | 21 |
| Sick, Christ healing the | 141 |
| Sight, Saul restored to | 251 |
| Sleeping, Jesus finds the Disciples | 91 |
| Sinned, Jerusalem hath | 87 |
| Sorcerer, Elymas the | 261 |
| Sower, the Parable of the | 151 |
| Star in the East, Wise Men and the | 5 |
| Starving, the Prodigal Son | 163 |
| Stephen, St. stoning of, to Death | 247 |
| Storm, Christ stilleth the | 15 |
| Spirit, Jesus casting out the Unclean | 59 |
| Spirits, Casting out the Unclean | 65 |
| Supper, the Last | 35 |
| Synagogue, Christ teaching in the | 137 |
| Tabitha, Peter raising | 253 |
| Tempted, Christ | 135 |
| Thomas, the Incredulity of | 227 |
| Thorns, Christ crowned with | 45 |
| Transfiguration, the | 27 |
| Viper, Paul shaking off the | 279 |
| Wilderness, Jesus in the | 133 |
| Widow's Son, Christ raising the | 147 |
| Woman, the Dragon persecuting the | 281 |
| Zacchæus, the Calling of | 173 |
| Zacharias, the Angel appearing to | 113 |

# THE SAVIOUR.

The words Jesus Christ, mean "the Saviour of the world," the word Messiah, has the same meaning as Christ.

It is not a little remarkable, that most of the nations of antiquity, however remote from Christianity, had a faith or superstition which exhibited many of the features of the religion of the Jews, as set forth in the Scriptures. They believed, that the world having been created and peopled with mortals, that gods and angels not unfrequently descended to earth and conversed with them. Presuming on this familiarity, men forgot their duty, offended their celestial visitants, who thereupon withdrew, and left them to their own evil ways. They greatly sinned, and then a mighty deluge punished their depravity, but some portion of the sinful men being spared, the world again became populous, and unhappily again became wicked. Their course in this advanced or second stage of depravity, became indeed so monstrous, that mercy could not be allowed to interpose her shield, and sacrifice was required. Thus it was that a Heavenly being, laying aside his inherent glory,

## THE SAVIOUR.

came to earth—he came to suffer that man should be spared. Such, in various myths, as they are called, or mythological fables, is made to appear the early history of man's creation, fall, punishment, relapse into vice, and final salvation through redeeming love.

We find here a confused and imperfect representation of those grand events on which depend the Christian's hope. They serve to prove the universality of the belief that man had fallen from a state of purity which was originally his; and that to snatch him from the consequences of his evil doings, the intercession of a gracious Mediator was held to be necessary.

Such a one was found. He, "the desired of all nations," appeared, but he came not in royal state. To give mortals an opportunity of manifesting disinterested love, he was born in poverty, and appeared before men as the son of a mean carpenter. It was by his deeds, by his words of wisdom and acts of charity, that the Son of the Almighty chose to manifest himself to the sons of men.

Children who are so happy as to have kind parents who supply all their wants, and keep them in peace and safety, may rejoice that their lot is so very different from that of the infant

MURDER OF THE INNOCENTS

# JOSEPH WARNED IN A DREAM.

"The angel of the Lord appeareth to Joseph in a dream, saying, Arise, and take the young child and his mother, and flee into Egypt, and be thou there until I bring thee word: for Herod will seek the young child to destroy him." —MATTHEW, chap. ii., verse 13.

---

THE warning God was pleased to give to Joseph of the wish of Herod to put the child Jesus to death, was not neglected. Joseph arose in the night, and took the infant and Mary his mother from Bethlehem in Judea, where they had previously rested, and set out for Egypt.

It will interest those who carefully read the Bible, to mark that Joseph was directed, in order to save the child from being destroyed, to repair to that land from which, in other days, Moses, by God's command, and under his benign protection, had rescued the Israelites from captivity. Egypt was a land wonderfully favoured in many respects. There, when famine involved the surrounding nations in great distress, abundance of corn was stored; there Jacob and his family found a home in the old age of the patriarch; and now, it was appointed to offer blessed refuge to the distressed earthly parents of the Saviour of the world.

Yet, strange as it is true, in that same Egypt

so little was the goodness of the Eternal valued or understood, that its inhabitants gave themselves up to the most shocking idolatry. Instead of bowing before the altar of the Lord; instead of offering homage to that gracious being who caused the river Nile to overflow, and bade the golden corn wave over its otherwise barren sands, they were content to prostrate themselves before monstrous images of stone, and even before senseless animals, and hateful reptiles. Such is the wretched abasement to which men condescend, who madly turn from the light, and indulge their own wild fancies instead of seeking to honour the true God.

Some of their huge idols have been brought to England; as works of art, or as curiosities, they may interest, but viewing them as objects before which man should prostrate himself in adoration, they can only be regarded as monuments of Egyptian folly.

# THE MURDER OF THE INNOCENTS.

"Then Herod, when he saw that he was mocked of the wise men, was exceeding wroth, and sent forth, and slew all the children that were in Bethlehem, and in all the coasts thereof, from two years old and under, according to the time which he had diligently enquired of the wise men."—MATTHEW, chap. ii., verse 16.

---

JOSEPH and Mary, with the child Jesus, had left Bethlehem, and were on their way to Egypt, when king Herod, who had waited in vain for the return of the wise men, found that they had gone to their home, and would not tell him what he wished to know. He was then very angry with them, and as he could not gratify his cruel nature by slaying the son of Mary alone, the wicked thought came into his mind, that by ordering all the poor little children in Bethlehem to be put to death, what he desired might be effected. He made sure that Jesus was among them, and cared not how much blood he shed, so the cause of his alarm were removed.

Then his wicked soldiers went and seized all the little boys and girls they could find in Bethlehem. Those hard-hearted men tore them from their helpless mothers. They cared

## THE MURDER OF THE INNOCENTS.

not for the cries of the children nor the prayers of their fond parents, but slew them all.

Dreadful was the scene Bethlehem p e-sented; but it realised what a holy prophet had long before told would take place, and " in Rama was there a voice heard, lamentation, and weeping, and great mourning, Rachel weeping for her children, and would not be comforted, because they are not."

When kind mothers are deprived of their children, in their deep affliction they at first can receive no comfort. The law of nature forbids them to hope that the lost ones will be restored in this world. They can only be soothed by the blessed assurances which they find in the Testament, that in his own time God, who " wipes the tear from all eyes," will remove their sorrow by death, and then, so they lead a pious life here, and live with becoming resignation to the will of their Eternal Father, they will at last rejoin their beloved infants in Heaven.

CHRIST TEMPTED.

# THE TEMPTATION OF CHRIST.

"The devil taketh him up into an exceeding high mountain, and showeth him all the kingdoms of the world, and the glory of them."—MATTHEW, chap. iv., verse 8.

AFTER THE BIRTH OF CHRIST, 30 YEARS.

SATAN, the Devil, is the great foe of man. Because for his rebellion and ingratitude he has been expelled from Heaven, where but for his wickedness he might have lived for ever, he seeks to make human beings his partners in misery. To this end he strives to tempt the good, and uses all his art to lead them into evil ways.

He was bold enough to try to impose upon the Son of God. Satan, fallen as he is, has still great power, and presumed to hope that he could prevail upon Christ to forget his Heavenly Father. He therefore carried Jesus to the top of a high hill or mountain, from which he could look down on all the kingdoms of this world. He could see their grandeur, their riches, and their glory. All these he promised to give to Christ, if he would consent to worship him.

But Jesus knew the tempter, and scorned both him and his offer. "Get thee hence, Satan," he said "for it is written, Thou shalt

## THE TEMPTATION OF CHRIST.

worship the Lord thy God, and him only shalt thou serve." Then the Devil left him.

Satan now often tries to make the good forget their duty. He shows them riches and worldly honours, and whispers to them that all these may be enjoyed, if they will lend themselves to falsehood and fraud. Too often he succeeds:

> "Blinded in youth, by Satan's arts,
> The world to our unpractised hearts
> A flattering prospect shows;
> Our fancy forms a thousand schemes
> Of gay delights and golden dreams,
> And undisturbed repose."

But let the young be assured vain, very vain, are all these tempting prospects. To be happy they must be good. All that can be gained by sin soon passes away, or becomes an evil:

> "Turns to sorrow shame and pain.

Let them bear in mind the words of our Lord to Satan, and remember that God only they must serve.

THE SERMON ON THE MOUNT

# THE SERMON ON THE MOUNT.

"And seeing the multitudes, he went up into a mountain: and when he was set, his disciples came unto him."—MATTHEW, chap. v., verse 1.

AFTER THE BIRTH OF CHRIST, 31 YEARS.

The disciples of Jesus gathered round their divine preceptor on a mountain, and there the Son of God deigned to teach them their duty.

And sweet and soothing were the words that fell from him. "Blessed," said he, "are the poor in spirit: for theirs is the kingdom of Heaven." Those who are humble here, are thus taught that happiness is reserved for them in a better world.

The Saviour continued, "Blessed are they that mourn: for they shall be comforted." Those who are here depressed by affliction, may look for comfort from God.

Further, he said, "Blessed are the meek: for they shall inherit the earth. Blessed are they which do hunger and thirst after righteousness: for they shall be filled. Blessed are the merciful: for they shall obtain mercy."

Thus it will be seen he taught his followers that meekness would have its reward; that mortals who seek to be good, shall not seek in

THE SERMON ON THE MOUNT.

vain; and that those who are merciful to others shall find mercy for themselves.

And "Blessed," he added, "are the pure in heart: for they shall see God. Blessed are the peacemakers: for they shall be called the children of God."

In this noble sermon we are taught the mission of our Lord. It was a mission of peace. He came not to destroy, but to purify and to save: he came to warn men against that strife to which they are sometimes betrayed by their evil passions. To calm these, to do their best to disarm rage, is the duty of the good, and the peacemakers shall be called the children of God.

Mercy and meekness, peace and purity, he wisely commends to all the sons of men. This ought not to be lost sight of in the world's rude strife. Great will be the reward of those who profit from his sage and gentle admonitions, for "the pure in heart shall see God;" though the meek and the righteous may suffer for a time, "theirs is the kingdom of Heaven."

CHRIST STILLING THE STORM

# CHRIST STILLETH THE STORM.

"And he saith unto them, Why are ye fearful, O ye of little faith? Then he arose, and rebuked the winds and the sea; and there was a great calm."—MATTHEW, chap. viii., verse 26.

AFTER THE BIRTH OF CHRIST, 31 YEARS.

THE disciples of Jesus were in a ship, the winds rose, and a storm raged. He was sleeping, but they were dreadfully frightened, and thought the ship would sink, and that they would all be drowned in the sea.

So they went to him and awoke him, and in their dismay cried, "Save, Lord: we perish."

These men, though instructed by Christ, and though he was present with them, still wanted courage. The roaring winds, and the agitated waves, filled them with vain alarm. Instead of manfully and serenely braving the danger, they seem to have given themselves up for lost; and despairingly exclaimed, "We perish."

Jesus looked on them with displeasure. "Why," said he, "are ye fearful, O ye of little faith?" He blamed them, but he relieved their fears, for "he arose, and rebuked the winds and the sea; and there was a great calm."

## CHRIST STILLETH THE STORM

In reading this remarkable history, we see a picture of the weak anxieties and foolish alarms to which men are prone to give themselves up.

The disciples looked at the tempest and abandoned hope. In an agony of terror their cry was, "We perish." How much suffering would they have been spared but for their little faith!

Let the lesson thus afforded never be forgotten. Great as the dangers may seem, deep as the gloom which surrounds us may be, the christian whose faith is firm, may calmly repose and defy the fury of the storm. He who came not to destroy, still lives; is competent to save those who humbly put their trust in him. While the man of the world weakly trembles and is filled with miserable fear, the Christian preserves his fortitude. He knows that he is in the hands of a gracious and Almighty father, and feels that he is secure, come what may, because he has faith in God.

TOUCHING THE HEM OF THE GARMENT.

# A WOMAN TOUCHES THE HEM OF CHRIST'S GARMENT.

"And, behold, a woman, which was diseased with an issue of blood twelve years, came behind him, and touched the hem of his garment."—MATTHEW, chap. ix., verse 20.

AFTER THE BIRTH OF CHRIST, 32 YEARS.

THE Saviour of the world, as presented to us in Scripture, proved his exalted dignity, not by exerting his power to control men, or to invest himself with those honours and possessions which ordinary mortals covet; but by reproving vice, doing good, and setting a bright example of spotless purity.

He did not reside in lordly halls, and revel in the luxuries which glad the rich. On the contrary, we find him constantly associated with the poor, enlightening their minds and abating their sorrows.

Those who were slow to believe in his divine mission, could not shut their ears to the fame of his great deeds. Among them was a woman who had been very ill for a number of years; she was meek and lowly, and did not dare to ask our Lord to relieve her pain. A worldly doctor she knew, with far less power than he possessed, would not give her such relief as

## TOUCHING THE HEM OF CHRIST'S GARMENT.

might be hoped from his skill, without fee or reward, and she had probably nothing to give.

But having heard of the wonderful works of Jesus, she resolved to watch his footsteps, and said within herself, this holy visitor is so full of virtue, that if I can but touch his garment I shall be well.

With this anxious hope, she approached him as he walked along, and touched only the hem of his dress. She did this as privately as possible, but the Saviour perceived it and turned round, asking who had done it.

The poor woman trembled, and was much frightened, but owned that the act was hers. Jesus kindly removed her fears, and told her not to be disturbed, for her faith had made her whole, and from that hour she was quite well.

Faith in the Saviour is thus shown to be all-sufficient to relieve distress. True christians constantly feel that,—

"The wounded conscience knows its power
The healing balm to give,
That balm the saddest heart can cheer,
And make the dying live."

# RAISING OF JAIRUS'S DAUGHTER.

"But when the people were put forth, he went in, and took her by the hand, and the maid arose."—MATTHEW, chap. ix., verse 25.

AFTER THE BIRTH OF CHRIST, 32 YEARS.

A STILL stronger proof of the power of faith than that already described, is furnished in the case of a young female, the daughter of a "certain ruler," named Jairus, who was reported to be dead.

Her father, in great distress, went to Jesus and told him that she was no more. He worshipped Christ, his child slept in death, but he felt assured that if the Lord would but lay his hand upon her, she would revive.

He was on his way to the ruler's house when the poor woman touched the hem of his garment. Arriving there he found minstrels assembled, according to the custom of that country, to perform a solemn or funeral service. Jesus told them that the daughter of Jairus was only sleeping. They were so convinced that she was really dead, that they not only doubted the truth of his declaration, but they even laughed at the Son of God. In the words of Saint Matthew, "they laughed him to scorn."

The folly of these scoffers was soon proved, Jesus approached the supposed corpse, took the maiden by the hand, and she immediately arose.

Self-sufficient men often believe that it is not in the power of God to make things other than they seem to their eyes. We ought to distrust ourselves. Jesus was not always to remain on earth, and miracles like those which he performed to prove to the beholders that his mission was from Heaven, we are not permitted to witness, but the record of them which has been preserved, should teach us that nothing is impossible to Him who made us. His goodness and his power know no bounds; his providence now often works mighty and unforeseen changes, and a day will come when wonders still more startling, will bring conviction of his greatness to all whose hearts may at present be inaccessible to truth.

CHRIST TEACHING FROM THE SHIP

# CHRIST TEACHING FROM THE SHIP.

"And great multitudes were gathered together unto him, so that he went into a ship, and sat; and the whole multitude stood on the shore."—MATTHEW, chap. xiii., verse 2.

AFTER THE BIRTH OF CHRIST, 32 YEARS.

THE simple eloquence of the Saviour of man, as well as the miracles he performed, caused many to attend him, who were not considered of the number of his disciples. They were attracted by admiring curiosity, some of them probably by a feeling less pardonable; but at all events crowds followed him.

On one occasion, to avoid the pressure, he passed into a ship, and thence addressed those who had gathered on the shore. He spoke to them in parables. That mode of teaching he adopted, because it was given to those more immediately connected with him "to know the mysteries of the kingdom of Heaven," though in some degree veiled, and to profit from his discourse, which scoffers could not understand.

From the ship he addressed the listeners and told this parable: a sower, when sowing his seed, dropped some of it by the way-side, when the fowls came and devoured

## CHRIST TEACHING FROM THE SHIP.

it; another portion fell on stony places, where there was not much earth, and this, when it sprung up was scorched and withered by the sun; while some fell among thorns, which choked it as it grew.

Such was not the case with all; one part of the sower's seed fell on good ground and in due time produced a noble harvest, some thirty, some sixty, and some a hundred-fold!

By this Christ is understood to have pictured the course of worldly men, in regard to divine knowledge. The good seed, that which truth and religion supply, is often dropped where it fails to take root. Cares which ought never to be allowed to interfere with our musings on eternity, in a manner consume it; present enjoyment causes the word as it were to wither in the mind, or growing troubles, when it is springing up, choke and cause it to be neglected or forgotten.

Blessed is he whose heart presents that good ground, in which the seed of eternal joy can fructify. Richly will it compensate the wise anxiety which duly tended it. Pious care will be largely requited, as in the case of the sower: nay still more magnificent the return—a brief season of virtuous labour will insure the pure-minded christian everlasting glory.

JESUS WALKING ON THE SEA.

# CHRIST WALKING ON THE SEA.

"And immediately Jesus stretched forth his hand, and caught him, and said unto him, O thou of little faith, wherefore didst thou doubt?—MATTHEW, chap. xiv., verse 31.

AFTER THE BIRTH OF CHRIST, 32 YEARS.

Jesus had sent his disciples to sea in a ship, and promised that he would follow. Left alone, he went apart on a mountain to pray. Meantime, a storm arose, and the ship in which the disciples were, met by contrary winds, was tossed about on the troubled ocean.

They were apparently in danger, and looked out in vain for their master till the fourth watch of the night, when they at length saw the form of a man walking on the sea. Their minds being disturbed before, so strange a sight filled them with fear. They thought it was a spirit.

Jesus observed their alarm, and was not slow to comfort his worshippers, but instantly called to them in these soothing words: "Be of good cheer; it is I; be not afraid."

Peter then answered the Saviour, and said: "Lord, if it be thou, bid me come unto thee on the water." Jesus replied, "Come;" and

## CHRIST WALKING ON THE SEA.

Peter left the ship to walk on the waves towards Christ. But the wind was boisterous, and he seemed about to sink; and, greatly alarmed, he cried, "Lord, save me."

Jesus promptly stretched forth his hand, caught the disciple, and, mildly reproving him, said: "O, thou of little faith! wherefore didst thou doubt?" Then both passed into the ship, and the storm subsided.

In the conduct of Peter, we see imaged that of many a faint-hearted Christian. Men believe they have made up their minds to follow Christ: but, when surprised by sharp trials, their courage fails, and they tremble for the immediate consequences.

But, in their distress, though their hearts should not be cast down, it is fitting that, like Peter, they should cry, "Lord, save me." Doing this, they find heavenly mercy is in reserve for them, and each may then apply to himself the kind rebuke of Jesus, "O thou of little faith, wherefore didst thou doubt?"

CHRIST AND THE WOMAN OF CANA

# CHRIST AND THE WOMAN OF CANAAN.

"And, behold, a woman of Canaan came out of the same coasts, and cried unto him, saying, Have mercy on me, O Lord, thou son of David; my daughter is grievously vexed with a devil."—MATTHEW, chap. xv.. verse 22.

AFTER THE BIRTH OF CHRIST, 32 YEARS.

A POOR woman called upon the Saviour to pity her because her child was afflicted, or, as it is expressed in the text, was "vexed with a devil."

The disciples of Jesus, who heard the complaint of the woman, having less compassion than their divine master, called to him to send her away. Christ reproved their want of feeling, and told them that he had been sent "unto the lost sheep of the house of Israel." To the supplicant he remarked, that "it was not right that the children's bread should be thrown to the dogs."

"Truth, Lord," she replied, "but yet the dogs eat of the crumbs which fall from their master's table."

This humble answer, joined as it was with a holy hope that divine goodness would grant her suit, proved all-sufficient. "O woman!"

## CHRIST AND THE WOMAN OF CANAAN.

Jesus exclaimed, "great is thy faith:" and her daughter was cured.

Happy, indeed, was this petitioner. The humility with which she pleaded, not to rank with the chosen followers of the Lord, but merely to be allowed access to the crumbs which fell from their tables—to receive that comfort of which they did not stand in need—and the faith manifested in the Son of God, gained her the boon she craved; and her child was restored.

A broken and a contrite heart obtains those blessings which the proud and the self-sufficient seek in vain. Hence the weak and the distressed are taught, that, in the day of their adversity, though humble their pretensions, they may boldly fly to the Redeemer for succour. The crumbs that fall from such a master's table are rich in celestial nourishment. While they abate present evils, they assure the sufferer that his sorrows shall soon cease for ever.

THE TRANSFIGURATION

# THE TRANSFIGURATION.

"Jesus was transfigured before them: and his face did shine as the sun, and his raiment was white as the light."—MATTHEW, chap. xvii., verse 2.

AFTER THE BIRTH OF CHRIST, 32 YEARS.

THE transfiguration of Christ brings a scene of great splendour before us. As was his habit, Jesus withdrew from the crowded haunts of men, taking with him "Peter, James, and John his brother," to "a high mountain." There we find, that, to the eyes of his wondering followers, he no more appeared like a mere mortal, as at other times he had done. He was transfigured; that is, on his human form celestial lustre was shed. He looked, it may be presumed, as he will be seen in heaven, for his face shone like the glorious orb of day.

Not only did the wondering disciples mark his unearthly aspect, but they saw, conversing with him, two holy servants of God, who long before had passed away in the ordinary course of nature.

Gazing on this sublime spectacle, Peter said, "Lord, it is good for us to be here: if thou wilt, let us make here three tabernacles; one

## THE TRANSFIGURATION.

for thee, and one for Moses, and one for Elias."

The disciple was still speaking, when a bright cloud overshadowed them, and a voice came out of the cloud, and said: "This is my beloved Son, in whom I am well pleased: hear ye him."

Struck with holy awe, the disciples fell on their faces; but Jesus dismissed their alarm, kindly touched them, and said, "Be not afraid," and then they found themselves with him alone. His late companions, Moses and Elias, had vanished.

The disciples were charged by the Lord not to make known the wonders they had seen, till he had risen from the dead. What had thus been revealed proved to them, and at the proper time was communicated by them to their fellow-disciples, and indeed to all mankind, that their gracious preceptor was really the Son of God, in whom his Almighty father was "well pleased."

CHRIST AND ZEBEDEE'S CHILDREN

# ZEBEDEE'S CHILDREN.

"Then came to him the mother of Zebedee's children with her sons, worshipping him, and desiring a certain thing of him."
MATTHEW, chap. xx., verse 20

### AFTER THE BIRTH OF CHRIST, 32 YEARS.

Two young men, the sons of a man named Zebedee, were among the followers of the Saviour. The mother, anxious for their eternal welfare, came to Christ, and entreated him to grant her a very great favour—that her children might sit, one on his right hand, the other on his left hand, when he should have entered into his kingdom of everlasting glory.

Jesus replied to her that she knew not what she asked. "Are ye," said he, "able to drink of the cup that I shall drink of, and to be baptized with the baptism that I am baptized with?"

The sons declared that they were able. Their being thus put forward gave offence to the other disciples. Jesus was a lover of peace. In his Sermon on the Mount he had told his disciples that blessed were the peace-makers; and he now hastened to calm the angry feelings which had been kindled. He reminded the angry brethren of the contentions which pre-

## ZEBEDEE'S CHILDREN.

vailed elsewhere among worldly-minded men; "but," said he, "it shall not be so among you; but whichsoever shall be great among you, let him be your minister, and whosoever will be chief among you, let him be your servant."

Here was a lesson for selfishness and pride! Jesus wished his disciples to know that humility exalts, and to feel that they best consult their own welfare, who study the interest and the happiness of others. This he enforced by his own example: the Son of Man, he told them, came "not to be ministered unto, but to minister," and even to give his life for the ransom of many. Pious men, women, and children, who hope to rejoice with him in heaven, it follows must be content to give themselves up to the performance of arduous and painful duties on earth. The sincere Christian will do well to bear constantly in mind what his master suffered, and be prepared to "drink of the cup" of sorrow from which he drank.

CHRIST RESTORING THE SIGHT TO THE BLIND.

# JESUS OPENING THE EYES OF THE BLIND.

"Jesus had compassion on them, and touched their eyes: and immediately their eyes received sight, and they followed him."—MATTHEW, chap. xx., verse 34.

AFTER THE BIRTH OF CHRIST 32 YEARS.

THE goodness of Jesus Christ had caused him to do so much to relieve virtuous sufferers, that wherever he moved, he was beset by the sick, the lame, and the blind.

Two blind men on one occasion presented themselves by the way-side. The bystanders told who was about to pass, and they immediately implored him to aid them, exclaiming, "Have mercy on us, O Lord, thou son of David."

These persons were in a crowd, and the multitude complained of them for thus calling on Jesus, and wished them to hold their peace; but they would not be restrained, and louder than ever was heard their cry of "Have mercy on us, O Lord, thou son of David."

The Saviour stopped, and turning toward them, enquired, what it was they wished that he should do to them. Their answer was, a humble entreaty that their eyes might be opened.

## JESUS OPENING THE EYES OF THE BLIND.

Moved with their suffering, and affected by their earnestness, Jesus had compassion on them. He touched their eyes, and the darkness in which they had pined was no more. "Their eyes received sight, and they followed him."

Many eminent divines, have applied their thoughts, and directed their eloquence, to the illustration of this passage in Christ's history. They have pointed out as worthy of imitation, the resolute importunity of the blind men. In vain the thoughtless multitude rebuked them, they cried out the more. Though at first unheeded, their perseverance was rewarded, and their sight was restored.

And hence we are taught that though the prayer of sorrow may for a season appear to be breathed in vain, supplicants ought not to be discouraged; ought not to turn aside in despair. Still pressing forward to the throne of grace, in his own good time, the All-wise may be pleased to grant their suit. The repetition of their cry accepted as evidence of their faith, their eyes will be opened, and they joyfully find their names enrolled among the accepted followers of Jesus.

CHRIST ENTERING JERUSALEM.

# CHRIST ENTERING JERUSALEM.

"A very great multitude spread their garments in the way; others cut down branches from the trees, and strawed them in the way."—MATTHEW, chap. xxi., verse 8.

AFTER THE BIRTH OF CHRIST 31 YEARS.

THE evangelist Matthew, furnishes a minute report of the entrance of Christ into Jerusalem. It is in more respects than one, truly interesting, not merely to the meditative Christian, but to general readers.

Having reached Bethphage, near the mount of Olives, Jesus thought it right to send forward two of his disciples to a neighbouring village, in which he told them they would find "an ass tied, and a colt." These his disciples were to loosen and take to him. He added, should any one question them about what they were doing, they were to say, "the Lord hath need of them."

All happened as he anticipated; the ass and her colt were found, brought to him, and an ancient prophecy was fulfilled, which ran thus, "Tell ye the daughter of Sion, behold, thy king cometh unto thee, meek and sitting upon an ass." The fame of Jesus as a prophet, was great. Crowds expected his coming, and

## CHRIST ENTERING JERUSALEM.

threw their garments and branches of trees in the road, in honour of their illustrious visitor.

At this period of his earthly course, Christ was popular. A very great multitude, we read, assembled to witness his arrival, yet he was content to enter the proud city of Jerusalem riding on an ass.

In the fifteenth century, when the Pope of Rome affected more than regal state, this was not forgotten by the reforming Christians of that era. Jerome of Prague, caused a pictorial representation of the Saviour entering Jerusalem, and the Pope progressing through Rome, to be produced and exhibited, as contrasts; to show how luxury and pride had seduced the prelate who claimed to be regarded as the successor of the followers of Christ, from that lowliness and sublime disregard of all that could flatter mortal vanity, which marked the course of "Him who came to seek his father's sheep in the wilderness."

The example set by Christ has in too many instances been strangely forgotten by those who wished to hold a distinguished rank among his followers. Jesus was a foe to pride, and wished those who aspired to rank with his disciples, to prove their fitness by humility, gentleness, and love.

THE LAST SUPPER.

# THE LAST SUPPER.

"Now when the even was come, he sat down with the twelve."—MATTHEW, chap. xxvi., verse 20

AFTER THE BIRTH OF CHRIST, 33 YEARS.

HISTORY presents us with nothing more affecting than the details of the last supper of Jesus Christ with his disciples.

He knew that his time was nearly come; preparations were made for the passover, and he sat down to the simple solemn festival with his twelve followers.

Had all been faithful, the scene would have been memorable; but it was rendered still more so, by the fact, then known to the Saviour, that one of those assembled around him was sordidly plotting, from love of gold, to betray him into the hands of cruel foes, that he might be mocked, tortured, and put to death.

Yet it was even so. He knew that one of them was to act this monstrous part, and pointed out the sinful individual.

How must Judas have trembled when he heard those peace-breathing lips, which seldom opened but to utter words of compassion, and suggestions of mercy, pronounce

## THE LAST SUPPER.

the dreadful sentence.—"Woe unto that man by whom the Son of Man is betrayed! it had been good for that man if he had not been born."

Jesus took the bread and brake it, and gave portions of it to his disciples, and he handed the wine cup to them, tenderly charging them to consider that the latter imaged his blood, which was to be "shed for the remission of sins."

He directed his disciples to do as they were then doing, to partake of bread and wine in communion, when he should be no more on earth, in tender remembrance of him their Teacher and friend, for he then declared that he would not drink thenceforth "of that fruit of the vine, until that day when he should drink it new with them in his Father's kingdom."

That touching and sorrowful repast, has since been constantly remembered in every Christian land. It is, of all the affecting observances of the Christian religion, the one which appeals most forcibly to the heart, recalling, as it does, what the Son of God said and did, when his firmness as a man was to be subjected to the last tremendous trial; when he was to render himself as "a sacrifice for all."

THE AGONY IN THE GARDEN

# CHRIST'S AGONY IN THE GARDEN.

"He went a little farther, and fell on his face, and prayed, saying, O my Father, if it be possible, let this cup pass from me: nevertheless not as I will, but as thou wilt."—MATTHEW chap. xxvi., verse 39.

AFTER THE BIRTH OF CHRIST, 33 YEARS.

IF our Lord, when he came on earth, had come in power—in that strength and greatness which originally belonged to him, it might be imagined that pains which would overcome an ordinary mortal, would in his case have been endurable. But the great work of man's salvation was not to be so easily performed; and Christ, while in the flesh, if he did not betray all the weakness, was subjected to all the painful sensibilities of man's nature.

We find this distinctly marked in the conversation which followed the last supper. "My soul," the illustrious victim sadly exclaimed, "is sorrowful even unto death."

By that time he and his disciples had reached a place or garden called Gethsemane. Then it was that he proved the depth of human sorrow. Dark images of the fiend-like barbarity to which he was about to be subjected, came over

## CHRIST'S AGONY IN THE GARDEN.

him, and in his agony he exclaimed, "O my Father, if it be possible, let this cup pass from me." How touching—how thrilling the cry! how intense must the pain have been which extorted it from the patient, all-enduring Jesus!

But the glorious sufferer did not stop there. In that moment of exquisite suffering, he added—"nevertheless not as I will, but as thou wilt."

Thus in his extremest grief, when most severely tried, the Redeemer, labouring under all the anguish that a mere mortal could know, set before us a shining example of utter self-abandonment—of prefect resignation to the will of his omnipotent father.

The Christian pilgrim as he advances through the rugged paths of life, when storms assail, and despondency overclouds the mind, will do well to recal what Christ suffered for him. A broken spirit in the hour of dismay, will naturally turn to its eternal source, and pray that the bitter cup may pass as Christ did, but let the sorrowing petitioner not forget to add, "nevertheless" O my father "not as I will, but as thou wilt."

CHRIST BETRAYED

# CHRIST BETRAYED.

"While he yet spake, lo, Judas, one of the twelve, came, and with him a great multitude with swords and staves, from the chief priests and elders of the people."—MATTHEW, chap. xxvi., verse. 47.

AFTER THE BIRTH OF CHRIST, 33 YEARS.

Jesus may be said to have been left alone in his woe. His disciples who had attended him to the garden, were overcome with weariness and grief—it could not be that they were indifferent to their master's distress—but when he had withdrawn from them only a short time, he found them asleep.

The prayer which he had addressed to God, he repeated a second and a third time, but always with the addition that not his will, but that that of his Almighty Father should be done. He felt that the great task he had taken upon himself must be performed, and prepared to undergo the last pang. He roused his sleepy companions, and announced to them that the betrayer was at hand.

Judas approached, accompanied by an armed multitude, who were to arrest the destined victim. That base-hearted man had before agreed with the men who were engaged to seize

## CHRIST BETRAYED.

Jesus, to point him out to them; "Whomsoever I shall kiss," said he, "that same is he: hold him fast."

The hostile band approached, and Judas advancing to Christ, accosted him in the language of reverential love, saying, "Hail master;" and then he kissed him.

The preconcerted signal given, Jesus was instantly secured, by those who attended for that purpose. That Jesus should be captured and should suffer, was necessary for the salvation of the world, and for the fulfilment of prophecy; but the treachery of Judas, we cannot contemplate without horror and disgust.

It is the duty of the youth who would have his name enrolled among the followers of the Lord, to shun violence and subdue rancour. He who cannot do this, has but ill-learned the lesson which it was the object of the Saviour to teach, for he set mankind an example of patience and mercy, but violence and rancour are less hateful than the monstrous perfidy of the vile Judas, who while smilingly regarding Jesus as a friend, and crying, "Hail master," could betray with a kiss.

PETER DENYING CHRIST

# PETER DENYING CHRIST.

"And after a while came unto him they that stood by, and said to Peter, Surely thou also art one of them; for thy speech bewrayeth thee. Then began he to curse and to swear, saying, I know not the man. And immediately the cock crew."—MATTHEW, chap. xxvi., verses 73 & 74.

AFTER THE BIRTH OF CHRIST 33 YEARS.

ONE of the primary objects of the Gospel, is to teach those who desire to rank among the followers of the Saviour, humility.

That humility which becomes a Christian, can only grow on a knowledge of the weakness of his nature. The disciple Peter, ardent and sincere in his devotion to Jesus, presumptuously declared, that though all beside should fall off from Christ, he would remain unmoved. He was immediately checked by Jesus, who told him, "before the cock crow thou shalt deny me thrice."

In a very short time this was proved. When cruel men reproachfully spoke to the disciple, and told him in an accusing tone, that he was known to be one of the followers of the persecuted Saviour, his courage failed him, his resolution gave way, and in his anxiety to escape from their anger or their scorn, he began

## PETER DENYING CHRIST.

to curse and swear, and said, "I know not the man." Scarcely were the words out of his mouth, when the cock crew. With grief and shame, the erring disciple then recalled what Jesus had foretold, and Saint Matthew writes, "he went out and wept bitterly."

In the conduct of Peter, we see how mournfully the good may swerve from duty. It should teach men not to be too confident. Because they mean well, it does not follow as a matter of course, that under all circumstances they will have the courage and presence of mind to do what is right. Let them try to fortify their good resolutions, and, unmoved by the frowns of men, be faithful to the truth, and to duty; be faithful to the end.

Failing to do this, weakly striving to escape blame or punishment, their hearts soon tell them they desire it. Then like Peter, they may weep bitterly. True repentance will, as in his case, obtain pardon, but the Christian must not be ashamed of his master here, if he hope to be owned by that master in heaven.

THE REPENTANCE OF JUDAS

# REPENTANCE OF JUDAS.

"Judas, which had betrayed him, when he saw that he was condemned, repented himself, and brought again the thirty pieces of silver to the chief priests and elders."—MATTHEW, chap. xxvii., verse 3.

AFTER THE BIRTH OF CHRIST, 33 YEARS.

Judas, who had been one of the followers of Jesus, who had enjoyed the privilege of conversing with the Son of God, and had been taught by him his duty, was wicked enough to betray him into the hands of the cruel Jews, who sought to put him to death.

Sinful men cannot escape punishment. Judas found this to his sorrow; the stings of conscience tortured him, and he could not enjoy the wages of guilt. In an agony of remorse, he took back the thirty pieces of silver, which he had received as the price of his crime, to the chief priest and the elders. He wished them to receive the money, and said he had sinned against innocent blood.

The hard-hearted men who had tempted him to his undoing, then looked on him with scorn, and mocked his distress. "What," said they, "is that to us? see thou to that."

He had performed the treacherous deed they

had desired to witness, and they cared not what the sad consequences might be to him. They rejoiced in the treason, but despised the traitor. Then the wretched man was truly miserable. He threw down the money in the temple, and, mad with grief, at seeing himself mocked by those whose favour he had hoped to gain, he went and hanged himself.

Ill-gotten money never fails to bring with it a curse. From youth to age, this solemn truth ought to be deeply engraved on every Christian's heart. All the luxuries, all the splendour, that wealth can command, are utterly worthless if he who possesses them wants peace of mind. The rich man who is conscious of crime, envies the humblest cottager, the meanest beggar, the most abject slave who has preserved his integrity. In the lordly hall, the wealthy wicked chief seeks for rest in vain; he lives in hopeless sorrow, and often, like Judas, dies by his own hand in despair.

CHRIST CROWNED WITH THORNS

# CHRIST CROWNED WITH THORNS.

" And when they had platted a crown of thorns, they put it upon his head, and a reed in his right hand: and they bowed the knee before him, and mocked him, saying, Hail King of the Jews!"—MATTHEW, chap. xxvii., verse 29.

AFTER THE BIRTH OF CHRIST, 33 YEARS.

IN our times, when a criminal is doomed to die, though he is proved to have stained his hands with blood, and is known to have committed a dreadfully aggravated murder, while contemplating the awful punishment which awaits him, generous pity is moved, soothing language is addressed to him, and men almost "forget his vices in his woe."

It was not so in the case of the Saviour of the world, who had been guilty of no crime. The unfeeling men who had power over him in his mortal state, were not content with condemning him to death on the cross. Brutal mockery was resorted to, and ingenious barbarity laboured to heighten his distress. Crowned with thorns, a reed was put into his right hand, as a sham sceptre; scoffers spit upon him, they smote him, and bending the knee

## CHRIST CROWNED WITH THORNS.

before him, they jeeringly affected to honour him by shouting, "Hail King of the Jews."

Nor was this all. Pretending to give him drink to allay his thirst, they offered him an odious mixture of vinegar and gall. He tasted it, but could not drink.

Then they crucified him. That mode of punishment was dreadful. A powerful writer in the *Quarterly Review*, says—"Of all the devices of cruel imagination, crucifixion is the masterpiece. The weight of the body was borne by a ledge projecting from the middle of the upright beam, and not by the hands and feet, which were probably found unequal to the strain. The frailty of man's frame comes at last to be its own defence; but enough remained to preserve the pre-eminence of torture to the cross. The process of nailing was exquisite torment, and yet worse in what ensued than in the actual infliction. The spikes rankled, the wounds inflamed, the local injury produced a general fever, the fever a most intolerable thirst; but the greatest misery to the sufferer was, while racked with agony, to be fastened in a position which did not permit him even to writhe."

Such were the torments endured by Christ.

THE TAKING DOWN FROM THE CROSS.

# CHRIST TAKEN FROM THE CROSS.

"And when Joseph had taken the body, he wrapped it in a clean linen cloth."—MATTHEW, chap. xxvii., verse 59.

AFTER THE BIRTH OF CHRIST, 33 YEARS.

WHEN at length the agonies of the Saviour had reached an end, when he had endured all that human nature could suffer, death, from which the happy and the thoughtless recoil with horror, brought the glorious victim repose. Relieved from consciousness and from pain, the mangled form of the Redeemer hung on the cross, when Joseph of Arimathea, a rich man, went to Pilate the governor, and begged that the body might be given to him. Pilate who had wished to save Jesus from his enemies, though he had not opposed their cruelty with proper resolution, granted his request.

The governor's consent obtained, Joseph took the body of our Lord from the cross, and wrapped it in a linen cloth. In that country it was common to commit the dead to the earth, not in a coffin, but in a winding-sheet. Thus the remains of Jesus were disposed of, and Joseph, with pious care, caused the corpse

## CHRIST TAKEN FROM THE CROSS.

to be deposited in a new tomb which had been hewed out for him in a rock. That done, he rolled a great stone to the door of the sepulchre and departed.

Joseph acted a kindly part. Pitying the dreadful inflictions which the victim of man's sin and of divine compassion had sustained, he in giving the corpse a grave, did all that charity in such circumstances could attempt, and placing a stone at the door of the sepulchre, of course it was his object to guard against the remains being disturbed by foolish curiosity, or ruffianly malice, which with impotent rage, will sometimes seek to pursue the fallen, even in the grave.

There it was his wish, in love for the departed, that the body should rest till reduced to dust, and for ever. He could hardly have anticipated what was soon to take place. Generous pity prompted him to act as he did, but would not have assured him of that grand consummation in which all Christians rejoice.

THE TWO MARYS

# THE TWO MARYS AT THE SEPULCHRE.

"And there was Mary Magdalene, and the other Mary, sitting over against the sepulchre."—MATTHEW, chap. xxvii., verse 61.

---

AFTER THE BIRTH OF CHRIST, 33 YEARS.

---

AFFECTION fondly lingers near the remains of the departed. The cynic may call this weakness, but he can hardly deny that it is nature.

Those moments, though mournful, are deeply interesting—

> "When by the bed of languishment we sit,
> Or o'er our dying friends in anguish hang,
> Wipe the cold dew, or stay the sinking head."

If sad the duty to perform, it is still a privilege which the kind relative or friend would not trust to another hand.

Such are the feelings awakened in virtuous believers, when in the course of nature an esteemed fellow-creature is called away. His good qualities are then industriously recalled, his faults, his weaknesses, are excused or forgotten, and the mourner is absorbed in generous sorrow.

If such the case when a man or woman dies of years, by gradual decay, it will easily be con-

## THE TWO MARYS AT THE SEPULCHRE.

ceived that great indeed must have been the sorrow of the two Marys, when they beheld, as Saint Mark tells us they did, "Looking on afar off," the dreadful spectacle on Mount Calvary. In the prime of life they saw their more than blameless friend and preceptor treated as the vilest criminal that ever sinned against divine or human laws. They knew him condemned to the most terrible anguish, yet they might not approach to "wipe the cold dew" from the pallid forehead, or to "stay the sinking head." Set up as a mark for cruel mockery, Jesus was left to expire in agony on the cross, while those who lamented his sufferings, were kept at a distance.

The awful scene at length closed. Human nature, which Christ had assumed, could sustain such dreadful inflictions no longer, and the Redeemer slept in death. Then it was the two Marys approached the dear remains of their Lord. They wept over those features which they had so often beheld lighted up by benevolence, instructing the ignorant, and relieving the afflicted, and when by the care of Joseph of Arimathea, the body had been placed in the rock, the two Marys, reluctant to withdraw, lingered near the door of the sepulchre.

THE RESURRECTION

# THE RESURRECTION OF JESUS.

"And, behold, there was a great earthquake: for the angel of the Lord descended from heaven, and came and rolled back the stone from the door, and sat upon it."—MATTHEW chap. xxviii., verse 2.

AFTER THE BIRTH OF CHRIST, 33 YEARS.

IT was on the night of Friday that the two mourners, the Marys, seated themselves near the door of the sepulchre, where it may be presumed they remained till daylight returned.

In the course of the Saturday, which was the Jewish sabbath, the chief priests and Pharisees entreated Pilate to set a watch over the body of Jesus, lest his disciples should steal it away, and report that he had risen from the dead. Pilate gave them permission to make it as secure as they could, and they, determined that none of his friends should have access to the corpse, put a seal on the stone, and set a watch to guard it.

These cares were vain. The angel of the Lord came from heaven and rolled away the stone, and seated himself thereon. Then the men appointed to keep watch, were filled with alarm, they trembled and swooned, or "became as dead men."

# THE RESURRECTION OF JESUS.

But to the two Marys, who at the close of the sabbath, had returned to the tomb, the angel brought words of comfort. "Fear not," said he, "I know ye seek Jesus, who was crucified. He is not here: come, see the place where the Lord lay. And go quickly, and tell his disciples that he is risen from the dead."

Christ had foretold that on the third day he should rise again, and this it was made the chief priests and Pharisees so anxious to guard against the remains being carried away.

For the two Marys, who had deplored with tears and heartfelt sorrow the tortures Jesus had to bear, what words can describe the joy, the emotion they must have felt, when a bright messenger from the sky gave them the glad tidings, that he whom they mourned as dead, had risen from the grave.

Often among the wise dispensations of Providence, we see the good mourn the loss of a kind and revered friend; but affection after a time, where faith is not wanting, receives an assurance almost as distinct as that given by the angel to Mary, that grief may be spared, that the loved ones removed, are not lost for ever, but have risen to happiness and Heaven.

ST. JOHN PREACHING

# SAINT JOHN PREACHING.

"The voice of one crying in the wilderness, Prepare ye the way of the Lord, make his paths straight."—MARK, chap. i., verse 3.

AFTER THE BIRTH OF CHRIST, 26 YEARS.

It had been revealed to the children of Israel long before the event, that the Messiah would visit this world. Holy and inspired seers, gifted to make known the future, proclaimed that a celestial guest might be expected. They moreover announced that a messenger should be sent before him to prepare the way.

And a voice was to be heard, the voice of one crying in the wilderness, "Prepare ye the way of the Lord, make his paths straight." That voice was the voice of John the Baptist. It was his mission to "preach the baptism of repentance for the remission of sins."

This eminent person was a pious man, whose habits were singular and austere. "John was clothed with camel's hair, and with a girdle of a skin about his loins; and he did eat locusts and wild honey."

John had a grateful task to perform. It was given to him to announce the speedy coming of the Saviour. In his preaching he told his

## SAINT JOHN PREACHING.

hearers of the exalted character of Christ, saying, "There cometh one mightier than I after me, the latchet of whose shoes I am not worthy to stoop down and unloose." "I indeed," said he, "have baptised you with water: but he shall baptise you with the Holy Ghost."

Christ came as the prophets had foretold. He was all that John had reported. But the Jews, though credulous enough to believe those who assured them that senseless images might be worthily worshipped, who taught them to bend the knee to such objects, and say, "these be thy gods, O Israel," could not put their trust in one whose piety and truth entitled him to confidence. Thus unhappily, foolish mortals, perverse and stubborn, obstinately shut their eyes, and will not see that which tends to their eternal benefit. Good men still cherish a hope that a day will come when "the paths of the Lord shall be made straight," and the truth beam on each benighted mind, with such resistless and appropriate glory, that all must give it a welcome.

ST. JOHN BAPTISING

# SAINT JOHN BAPTIZING.

"It came to pass in those days, that Jesus came from Nazareth of Galilee, and was baptized of John in Jordan."—MARK, chap. i., verse 9.

AFTER THE BIRTH OF CHRIST, 30 YEARS.

HE who was appointed to be the forerunner of the Redeemer, the chosen herald of the Son of God, was permitted to receive a still greater honour, that of performing the baptismal ceremony for Christ.

John had been engaged in preaching baptism and the remission of sins, when Jesus left Nazareth and repaired to him to be baptized in the river Jordan.

It is not too much to suppose that one who had been apprized of the coming of the Lord, and appointed to prepare his ways, was not unacquainted with the quality of that communicant who now appeared before him; yet even a knowledge of his character and high mission, could hardly have prepared him for the wonders which were to be seen and heard on that great day.

The ceremony had been completed, not as it is usually performed now, but in the open river, and John had left the water, when he saw

## SAINT JOHN BAPTIZING.

the heavens open, and the holy spirit in the form of a dove, descending upon Jesus!

It was impossible for the Baptist to gaze on such a grand and extraordinary spectacle, but with breathless amazement and awe. It was still before his eyes, when a voice was heard from heaven, it was that of the Almighty himself, addressed to the Saviour, and saying, "Thou art my beloved Son, in whom I am well pleased."

Jesus, at this time, as a mortal, had reached maturity. He had commenced, or was about to commence, his grand labour, and to undergo his fiery trial, which, it is generally believed, he was not to enter upon till he had passed through youth to manhood. "The praise and love breathed on him from the sky," as recorded by the evangelist Mark, by his great and Eternal Father, was therefore the reward of a virtuous and blameless life, up to that moment.

Youthful readers perusing the eventful story of the Son of God, are to remember that he had all the weaknesses of humanity, while he was here. Yet he was pure, and his dread Sire "in him was well pleased." It is quite possible for his followers to imitate his purity, if with unbending faith they seek to share his everlasting glory.

SIMON AND ANDREW CALLED BY JESUS

# SIMON AND ANDREW CALLED BY JESUS.

"As he walked by the sea of Galilee, he saw Simon and Andrew his brother casting a net into the sea: for they were fishers. And Jesus said unto them, Come ye after me, and I will make you to become fishers of men."—MARK, chap. i., verses 16 & 17.

AFTER THE BIRTH OF CHRIST, 30 YEARS.

In the Old Testament, we read, that when presumptuous men undertook to erect a building which should reach to the sky, their daring folly was requited by their being thrown into helpless embarrassment, from the confusion of tongues. Their enterprise was rendered a total failure, by the will of Him to whose dwelling they had insolently proposed to ascend, in the vain hope that doing so, would save them from future danger.

To humble pride, has ever been the will of the Almighty. Disdain for the proud of this world, is evinced by the Saviour. Those who in their own conceit, were most eminent for piety, or for learning, he valued not, but to raise the lowly, and give them dignity and importance, was his pleasure.

In the case of the arrogant builders of Babel,

## SIMON AND ANDREW CALLED BY JESUS.

the power of making themselves understood was taken from them; in that of the untaught followers of the Lord, an extraordinary gift of language was vouchsafed to them, which rendered their speech intelligible, where before they had no means of giving utterance to their thoughts.

Such was the miraculous power of Jesus, that he could qualify the ignorant to teach, while he confounded the worldly-wise.

When walking by the sea of Galilee, he saw Simon and Andrew, two poor fishermen, casting their nets; he knew they were not scholars, that they were not possessed of learning, but he called to them to follow him, and he would make them fishers of men. By this he meant that unlettered as they were, he would enable them to snatch men from the sea of iniquity, in which they were immersed, and render them the messengers of mercy to their fellow-creatures.

Divine illumination, no doubt, came instantly over their minds at the call of Jesus. They forsook their nets, and followed him: they abandoned earthly cares, to fix their thoughts on Heavenly glory.

# JESUS CASTING OUT THE UNCLEAN SPIRIT.

"And there was in their synagogue a man with an unclean spirit; and he cried out."—MARK, chap. i., verse 23.

AFTER THE BIRTH OF CHRIST, 30 YEARS.

JESUS taught "as one that had authority, and not as the Scribes" had been accustomed to teach, and throughout his mortal pilgrimage, he was found giving the most important lessons in a style and manner peculiarly his own, and proving that he "had authority, by the wonders he performed."

He was teaching in the synagogue at Capernaum when a man was presented to him who was troubled with an unclean spirit.

This spirit, St. Mark reports to have cried out, saying, "Let me alone; what have we to do with thee, Jesus of Nazareth? Art thou come to destroy us? I know thee, who thou art, the Holy One of God."

Jesus rebuked him, saying, "Hold thy peace, and come out of him."

The command, we read, was not issued in vain, for the Evangelist goes on, "When the unclean spirit had torn him (the sufferer), and

## JESUS CASTING OUT THE UNCLEAN SPIRIT.

cried with a loud voice, he came out of him. And they (the bystanders) were all amazed, insomuch that they questioned among themselves, saying, what thing is this; what new doctrine is this?"

They were astonished, as well they might be, to find that the speaker had power over unclean spirits, who were compelled to obey him. It was, indeed, an extraordinary case, in which one so meek, so gentle, as Jesus was in his general course of life, proved that he had at his command such irresistible power, that devils perceiving him, were compelled to tremble and depart at his bidding.

This the Jews had an opportunity of knowing, and in consequence, the Saviour's fame was spread abroad, through all the region round about Galilee. It was known that he was potent to relieve those who were afflicted, and many were sufficiently on the alert to resort to resort to him, that their maladies might be cured. If men were as careful to seek Heaven as they are to crave relief from present anguish, the Saviour's gracious call would not be often neglected.

THE LEPER CLEANSED

# THE LEPER CLEANSED.

"There came a leper to him, beseeching him, and kneeling down to him, and saying unto him, If thou wilt, thou canst make me clean."—MARK, chap. i., verse 40.

AFTER THE BIRTH OF CHRIST 31 YEARS.

In consequence of that fame, which has already been spoken of, which Jesus gained as one who could heal the sick, a leper came to him, and entreated him to make him clean.

Among the Jews a leper was regarded with great horror. We see in the Bible that even a king was no more respected when he was afflicted with leprosy. Not only suffering pain, but despised by his fellow-men, who might have been expected to sooth his distress, the case of the leper was most pitiable. Happily he applied to one who, in a case of real woe, it was not difficult to move. Jesus compassionately "put forth his hand and touched him, and saith unto him, I will; be thou clean."

More was not necessary. No sooner had the Saviour uttered these few words, than the leprosy departed from the sufferer, and he was clean.

When he was going, Jesus said to him, "See thou say nothing to any man; but go

## THE LEPER CLEANSED.

thy way, show thyself to the priest, and offer for thy cleansing those things which Moses commanded, for a testimony unto them."

The man, however, did not heed what the Saviour said to him in this instance. He went forth and published it, or, as Mark tells us, "began to blaze abroad the matter."

The consequence was, that multitudes went to Jesus from every quarter, so that he could no longer go about the city. He then withdrew into the desert, but even there they seem to have followed him. To him who could heal their bodily ailments, and did it too, without expense, they were willing to resort in crowds.

The case of the leper evinces the importance of faith in the goodness of the Saviour. There is a leprosy of the mind as well as of the body. Let him who is afflicted with the former imitate the leper of Galilee, and call for aid from above, in the full conviction that the Lord who hears the sinner's prayer can make him clean.

# CHRIST HEALING ONE SICK OF THE PALSY.

"They came unto him bringing one sick of the palsy, which was borne of four."—MARK, chap. ii., verse 3.

AFTER THE BIRTH OF CHRIST, 31 YEARS.

Jesus having returned to Capernaum, a poor man who was afflicted with the palsy was brought to him, being borne into his presence by four persons. The crowds which his previous miracles had caused to follow him were so great, that the friends of the sick man could not get through to the Saviour; but resolute to gain their point, they unroofed the house in which he rested, and let down the bed on which the sick man was prostrate, from the top of the building.

This mark of faith in his goodness was graciously noted by Christ, and he said to the sick man, "Son, thy sins be forgiven thee."

Certain scribes were sitting near, and took upon themselves to say, "Why doth this man speak blasphemies? Who can forgive sins but God only?"

Jesus asked why they reasoned thus, and whether it was easier to say to the sick of the

## CHRIST HEALING ONE SICK OF THE PALSY.

palsy, "Thy sins be forgiven thee," or to say, "Arise, and take up thy bed and walk?" Their looks, or words, doubtless intimated, that the one might be done, but the other was impossible.

And then, that they might know that the Son of Man had power on earth to forgive sins, to convince them that he could do more than speak, or speak with more effect than other men, he said, addressing his speech to the sick man, "Arise, and take up thy bed, and go thy way into thine house."

The important word was spoken, and immediately the sufferer, now a sufferer no more, arose, took up his bed and went forth before them all.

This wonderful sight astonished the beholders, and St. Mark adds, they "glorified God." All doubt that he who could thus chase disease before him, came from the Most High, vanished. They exclaimed, anything like what was then witnessed they had never seen before. On their minds no doubt remained. The divine power was too gloriously displayed not to carry conviction to the hearts of those who had dared at first to declare that the Redeemer uttered blasphemies.

CASTING OUT THE UNCLEAN SPIRIT

# CASTING OUT THE UNCLEAN SPIRITS.

"And forthwith Jesus gave them leave, and the unclean spirits went out and entered into the swine; and the herd ran violently down a steep place into the sea (there were about two thousand,) and were choked in the sea."—MARK, v. 13.

AFTER THE BIRTH OF CHRIST 30 YEARS.

WE find in the Gospel of St. Mark, a wonderful relation of a miracle wrought by Jesus. The Evangelist reports, that our Lord being in the country of the Gadarenes, was met by one who was troubled with an unclean spirit. This man, strange to tell, had his dwelling among the tombs. So disturbed was he in his mind, that he was very violent, and withal so strong, that no one could effectually restrain him, for when bound with chains and fetters, which would have rendered any other man helpless, he brake them in pieces.

Night and day this wretched mortal ran about in a distracted manner, sometimes wandering on the mountains, and at others raving among the tombs. His cries were loud and dismal, and he often cut his flesh with sharp stones.

The poor man seeing the Saviour at a dis-

## CHRIST CASTING OUT THE UNCLEAN SPIRITS.

tance, ran and worshipped him. Jesus pitying his distress, commanded the unclean spirit, or rather the unclean spirits, for there were many, and their name was Legion, to come out of the sufferer. His awful voice filled the evil ones with terror, and they prayed him to let them take possession of a herd of swine. He permitted them to do so, and and the swine, about two thousand in number, ran into the sea, where they were drowned.

The man was happily cured, and was sent home by Jesus, to make known what the Lord had done for him. By becoming a devout worshipper of Christ, a frantic maniac was restored to reason, and his affliction, long deemed hopeless, was no more.

The sufferer so relieved was but a type of the man who long pining in spiritual darkness is at length brought to know the truth. His happiness is great who feels that his peace is made; it fades not with the common enjoyments of life, but defies the assaults of age, sickness, and death.

JOHN THE BAPTIST'S HEAD BROUGHT ON A CHARGER.

# JOHN THE BAPTIST'S HEAD BROUGHT IN A CHARGER.

"And immediately the king sent an executioner, and commanded his head to be brought; and he went and beheaded him in the prison, and brought his head in a charger."—MARK, chap. vi., verses 27, 28.

AFTER THE BIRTH OF CHRIST, 30 YEARS.

JOHN THE BAPTIST, it has already been seen, was enabled to make known that the Saviour of the world was at hand. Austere in his life, and virtuous in his habits, he zealously opposed sin, and feared not even to reprove a monarch who had married the wife of his brother.

The name of the lady was Herodias, and she was very angry with John for saying what a sense of duty prompted, and the wicked woman longed for revenge.

An oportunity soon offered for gratifying her malice. Her daughter danced before the king, and he was so immoderately pleased with what he saw, that he told her he would give her anything she might desire, even to the half of his kingdom. The foolish promise he confirmed with an oath.

The daughter went to her mother to seek advice as to what she had better ask, and

### THE BAPTIST'S HEAD BROUGHT IN A CHARGER.

Herodias, thirsting for the blood of the pious man who had blamed her depravity, desired the daughter to pray Herod that the head of John the Baptist might be brought to her.

Upon that she went unto Herod and said, "I will that thou give me by and by, in a charger, the head of John the Baptist." Herod was reluctant to comply with the monstrous wish, but bound by an oath, he thought he must not refuse, and accordingly he sent an executioner to behead the Baptist in prison, and his head was brought to the damsel, who gave it to her cruel parent. What frightful depravity to prefer to a beautiful present, the ghastly bleeding head of a murdered man!

Beware of rash oaths. Through madly swearing where no oath was necessary, Herod was led to stain his hands with the blood of a pious monitor.

JESUS FEEDS THE MULTITUDE.

# JESUS FEEDS THE MULTITUDE.

"When he had taken the five loaves and the two fishes, he looked up to heaven, and blessed, and brake the loaves, and gave them to his disciples to set before them, and the two fishes divided he among them all."—MARK, chap. vi., verse 41

AFTER THE BIRTH OF CHRIST, 30 YEARS.

THE wonders wrought by Jesus caused a multitude to follow him. Having withdrawn with some of his disciples to a desert, and being thus attended, the day was nearly spent, and the crowd were faint and weary.

His disciples proposed sending them away, that they might buy bread for themselves, but Christ desired that food should be given to them. They seemed to raise an objection to this, and said, "Shall we go and buy two hundred pennyworth of bread, and give them to eat?"

To this question he replied by asking how many loaves they had, and being answered, "Five loaves and two fishes," he caused them to be brought to him; and then commanding those around to sit down in companies on the grass, when they were collected in hundreds and in fifties, "he looked up to heaven, and blessed and brake the loaves, and gave them to

## JESUS FEEDS THE MULTITUDE.

his disciples to set before the hungry people, and the two fishes divided he among them all."

The multitude, consisting of five thousand persons, "ate and were filled," and afterwards the fragments remaining filled twelve baskets.

Than this nothing can be more astonishing. But the Creator who made the loaves and the fishes, to prove before men the true character of the Saviour, was pleased on this occasion thus to increase the store of food in his hands. Christ knew to whom he appealed for aid, and knew that to his Almighty Father nothing is impossible. To entertain a doubt of this is folly. Was thus furnishing the means of feeding a multitude, more wonderful than the creation of a world? Can it be doubted that the world was created? Doubting of this, it would puzzle a scoffer to account for what he sees, and even for his own existence.

CHRIST RESTORES SIGHT TO THE BLIND MAN

# CHRIST RESTORES SIGHT TO THE BLIND MAN.

"And he cometh to Bethsaida, and they bring a blind man unto him, and besought him to touch him. And he took the blind man by the hand, and led him out of the town; and when he had spit on his eyes, and put his hands upon him, he asked him if he saw ought."—MARK, chap. viii., verses 22, 23.

AFTER THE BIRTH OF CHRIST 30 YEARS.

If the Evangelists, in their several narratives, present some repetitions, they also give important corroboration of some of those astonishing facts which occurred in the history of the Saviour, which, if not necessary, is still not undesirable.

At a place called Bethsaida we read a blind man being brought to Christ was restored to sight. When thus favoured, in reply to a question which Jesus put to him, he looked up, and said he saw men, and to him they appeared like trees walking. "The Lord," after that, "put his hands again upon his eyes, and made him look up; and he was restored, and saw every man clearly."

The cure being thus perfected, the man was sent to his home, but with a charge not to tell of it in the town where he resided.

## CHRIST RESTORES SIGHT TO THE BLIND MEN.

In several cases, where sufferers had been relieved by the Lord, they were dismissed with this admonition. Sometimes, in proof of the power which the Father confided to him, astonished thousands were permitted to witness such deeds as never man performed; at others the object of the benevolent Jesus was only to relieve individual distress, to set an example of doing good in secret.

The imperfect vision of the poor man when he first gained sight, some able divines have likened to the mental wanderings which some Christians have known when first their hearts were accessible to sacred truth; and the clearness with which he afterwards saw objects as they really were, to the rapid advances of the understanding marked in those who continue to seek truth by the light of Scripture.

CHRIST DISPUTING WITH THE PHARISEES.

# CHRIST DISPUTING WITH THE PHARISEES.

"And the Pharisees came to him, and asked him, Is it lawful for a man to put away his wife? tempting him."—MARK, chap. x., verse 2.

AFTER THE BIRTH OF CHRIST, 31 YEARS.

THE Pharisees, a self-sufficient body, were much disposed to treat the Saviour with scorn. To show their own fancied superiority, they often engaged him in argument, but the result always forcibly rebuked their vanity.

They came, St. Mark writes, "tempting him," when he was in Judea, by inquiring whether he held it to be "lawful for a man to put away his wife?"

Our Lord, in answering these proud and artful men, applied himself to impress upon them, and upon all men, in what reverence the marriage tie ought to be held.

From the beginning of the world, he told them, God having created male and female, designed them to come together, and being united, it became the duty of a man to "leave his father and mother and cleave to his wife."

Children will not from this understand that when grown up to be men, they are to desert or treat parents with unkindness. That, the Saviour never taught; but he spoke of the intimate union of man and wife, as above all things to be respected. "Those," said he, "whom God hath joined, "let no man put asunder."

Thus delivering himself, Christ meant to warn men against creating discord between persons joined in marriage. He wished men to feel, that to defend, to cherish, and sustain their wives, was their first duty, a duty with which no claim ought to be permitted to interfere. It is especially desirable, that from earliest youth this feeling should "grow with our growth, and gain strength with our strength." All who are near to us are to be loved, but none so steadfastly, none so dearly as a wife.

Whatever the Pharisees might argue from the old law, the marriage state was honoured by the Saviour, and the union declared to be that which no man ought to seek to dissolve.

CHRIST BLESSING LITTLE CHILDREN

# CHRIST BLESSING LITTLE CHILDREN.

"But when Jesus saw it he was much displeased, and said unto them (the disciples), Suffer the little children to come unto me, and forbid them not, for of such is the kingdom of God."—MARK, chap. x., verse 14.

AFTER THE BIRTH OF CHRIST, 31 YEARS.

IN most of the scenes in which Christ is seen with his disciples, the master is distinguished from the servant not by his proud and stately carriage, but by his superior gentleness.

This was especially seen on one occasion, when little children were brought to him, that he might teach them. His disciples looked on them with some unkindness, and rebuked or found fault with those who brought them.

Not such was the conduct of Jesus. We are distinctly told that he was much displeased with his disciples, for their churlish behaviour, and he immediately called to them, "Suffer little children to come unto me, and forbid them not;" adding, "for of such is the kingdom of God."

Then he took the little ones "up in his arms, put his hands upon them, and blessed them."

Nor was this all, for he taught his followers

## CHRIST BLESSING LITTLE CHILDREN.

that they, if they would enter into God's kingdom, must become as little children. His words were these: "Verily, verily, I say unto you, whosoever shall not receive the kingdom of God as a little child, shall not enter therein."

Intelligent, well-disposed young students reading this, will hardly need to be told how largely they are favoured. Can they desire greater honour, than to know their parents must become like children to gain Heaven? To preserve the innocence which is theirs should be their anxious care in after life. It is their duty, and it is beyond all doubt their interest. They will not neglect it if they are duly grateful to their divine preceptor. Let them ever bear in mind the condescending kindness and love of him who could take children in his arms, bless them, and proclaim that "of such is the kingdom of God."

CHRIST RESTORING SIGHT TO BARTIMEUS

# CHRIST RESTORING SIGHT TO BARTIMÆUS.

"And they came to Jericho: and as he went out of Jericho with his disciples and a great number of people, blind Bartimæus, the son of Timæus, sat by the highway side begging."—MARK, chap. x., verse 46.

AFTER THE BIRTH OF CHRIST, 30 YEARS.

THE Son of God having visited Jericho, as he was leaving that city, attended by his disciples and followed by a crowd, a beggar, named Bartimæus, sat by the highway. He was told that Jesus of Nazareth was passing, upon which he raised his voice, and called out, "Jesus, thou Son of David, have mercy upon me."

Many who heard the poor man cry out, told him to hold his peace; but he cried the more a great deal, "Thou Son of David, have mercy upon me."

Happy it was for him that he did so, for Jesus stood still, and commanded him to be called. Those near Bartimæus, upon this, bid him "be of good cheer, for he was called."

He stood before Christ, who then demanded, "What wilt thou that I shall do unto thee?

## CHRIST RESTORING SIGHT TO BARTIMÆUS.

The blind man said unto him, "Lord, that I might receive my sight."

The poor beggar was answered as others had been under somewhat similar circumstances, "Go thy way, thy faith hath made thee whole." He then became one of the followers of Jesus.

Great was his happiness to be relieved from the blindness which he had long deplored, and the mighty benefit was owing to his resolutely continuing to call on the Lord. The example set by Bartimæus is worthy of universal imitation. Let the sufferer who wants Divine aid, persist humbly and earnestly to press his suit. It is weakness to suppose the Eternal must immediately attend at our bidding. We must patiently, though anxiously wait his good pleasure. Though thoughtless men should bid him hold his peace, or even tell him prayer is useless, he must not attend to them, but still call on "the Son of David," in the full conviction that he will not always call in vain.

CHRIST CURSETH THE BARREN FIG TREE.

# CHRIST CURSES THE BARREN FIG-TREE.

"And seeing a fig tree affar off having leaves, he came, if haply he might find any thing thereon: and when he came to it, he found nothing but leaves; for the time of figs was not yet. And Jesus answered and said unto it, no man eat fruit of thee hereafter for ever."—MARK, chap. xi., verses 13, 14.

AFTER THE BIRTH OF CHRIST, 31 YEARS.

SUBJECTED to all the wants of humanity, we read the Son of God, being come from Bethany, saw a fig-tree, and suffering from hunger, he approached it, with a view of partaking of its fruit. When he came to it, he found the tree was barren. Those who live in modern times, in great civilized communities, know little of the necessities which the sons of men experienced in earlier days. They did not look on rows of shops, amply stocked with all the necessaries and luxuries which all the countries on the face of the globe could furnish, but were obliged to turn to the fields and the trees for such a supply as nature, unassisted by skill and science, might offer, and when these failed, distressing want, and indeed starvation, stared them in the face.

Christ saw the fig-tree presented nothing

that could satisfy the appetite of man, and then he doomed the tree to remain in the same state thenceforth and for ever.

Holy men have laboured to inprove this incident. The barren fig-tree, which carried no fruit at the proper season, on which the cheering beams of the sun, and the refreshing shower had fallen in vain, they liken to the human being, who favoured in the course of nature by all that ought in due time to produce virtuous resolution and good actions, is still found wanting. On such they have inferred the sentence pronounced against the worthless tree must fall. A day lost cannot be recalled, and the consequences may be terrible. This night thy soul may be required of thee. Having failed at the right period to give what might be expected, they are cut off from the hope of flourishing as they might have done in the time to come. The wise and pious youth musing on this will see, that " now is the appointed time," that the present moment madly neglected, the immortal soul may be lost for ever.

CHRIST CASTING OUT THE MONEY CHANGERS

# CHRIST CASTING OUT THE MONEY-CHANGERS.

"Jesus went into the temple, and began to cast out them that sold and bought in the temple, and overthrew the tables of the money-changers, and the seats of them that sold doves."
—Mark, chap. xi., verse 15.

After the Birth of Christ, 31 years.

As we trace the progress of Christ, how often are we compelled to admire his gentleness, humility, and benevolence! It is only in this instance, in the case described in the text quoted above, that we find him moved to violence. His was not the wrathful disposition, nor his the wretchedly irritable nature that could not mark error without visiting it with severe resentment; he could patiently rebuke, mildly admonish, and strive by kindness to reform.

What was it moved his indignation in this case? It was, that on coming to Jerusalem, and entering the Temple, he saw the house of God profaned by lovers of money. Their greedy doings caused him to lay aside his usual meekness. With courage and resolution equal to his goodness, he assailed the worshippers of gold, and overthrew the tables of some and the seats of others, and several he turned out of the building.

The feeling which prompted him was this: he knew that men could not serve God and Mammon, and disgusted with the movements of avarice which met his eyes, within walls consecrated to the Lord of all, he scrupled not at once to put a stop to the unholy traffic, while he demanded, "Is it not written, my house shall be called of all nations, the house of prayer?" Adding the sharp reproach, "but ye have made it a den of thieves."

Yet, notwithstanding this stern reproof of such practices, in subsequent years, men who claimed credit for piety, and proclaimed themselves followers of Jesus, as eagerly sought wealth in "the house of prayer," as the money-changers did, or the sellers of doves. Surely some of them must, in their last moments, have been visited with the keenest pangs of remorse, for having, so far as in them lay, made the temple of the Lord little better than a den of thieves.

# THE TRIBUTE MONEY.

"And he saith unto them, whose is this image and superscription? And they said unto him, Cæsar's."—MARK, chap. xii., verse 16.

AFTER THE BIRTH OF CHRIST, 31 YEARS.

THE great reforms which Christ advocated, caused many who profited by the abuses which he anxiously laboured to put down, to plot against him. That he should condemn their hypocrisy, interfere with their unholy gains, and throw them into the shade by the wonderful deeds which he performed, were in the eyes of wicked selfish men, crimes not to be forgiven. The reflections he, in his parables, had cast upon them, made some of them very angry, and they determined, if they could, to prove that he was disaffected to the government. Severally the Pharisees and Herodians were accordingly moved, to attempt drawing from him some incautious speech, which they might use to his prejudice, as the foundation of a serious charge against him. They spake to him in an artful wheedling manner, and said, "Master, we know that thou art true and carest for no man, for thou regardest not the person of men, but teachest the way of God in truth. Is it lawful to give tribute to Cæsar or not? Shall we give, or shall we not give?"

Jesus saw the object of these treacherous men, through their pretended admiration. "Why," said he, tempt ye me? Bring me a penny, that I may see it."

One was brought to him, and looking at the coin, he then asked whose image and superscription it bore? They could do no other than answer, "Cæsar's." "Then," he replied, "Render unto Cæsar the things that are Cæsar's, and to God the things that are God's."

This answer confounded those who had sought to ensnare him. The tribute the Saviour claimed for God, was not what was necessary to the splendour of a worldly monarch. His followers, while they worship the King of Kings, do not cease to be loyal subjects to those whom it has been his good pleasure to set in authority over them. To Cæsar they give what is due to Cæsar, to the Almighty what belongs to God.

# THE WIDOW'S MITE.

"Jesus sat over against the treasury, and beheld how the people cast money into the treasury: and many that were rich cast in much."—MARK, chap. xii., verse 41.

AFTER THE BIRTH OF CHRIST, 31 YEARS.

THE simple and affecting incident connected with the widow's mite, has been admired by many generations of men. While Jesus remained in Jerusalem, his attention was drawn to those who threw money into the treasury.

It appears that the rich gave liberally, but there came a certain poor widow, and she only threw in two mites, which made a farthing.

The offering was poor, in a worldly point of view, but our Lord calling to his disciples, spake to them, thus: "Verily, I say unto you, that this poor widow hath cast more in than all which they have cast into the treasury; for all they did cast in of their abundance; but she, of her want, did cast in all that she had, even all her living."

By this striking commentary, we are taught God is not a sordid Deity, who covets what mortals deem wealth, and finds no offering acceptable but that which is costly and superb. The tribute which the meanest, poorest, man,

## THE WIDOW'S MITE.

woman, or child can render, however small its monetary value, bearing a just proportion to the giver's means—if it be an offering from the heart—will not be scorned. The two mites of the poor widow, as they were all she had, were held by Christ to be of more value than the showy donations of her wealthy neighbours; and if, as a modern writer remarks, the bereaved one had only been able to offer a tear, (compassionating another's woe) it would have been deemed sufficient to recommend her to the favourable notice of Divine benevolence.

The Searcher of all hearts sees the acting motives of men. Does pomp make a showy offering? That is not charity. The unassuming humility which gives without a thought of praise, is that which gains the approving smile of God.

# JERUSALEM HATH SINNED.

"And Jesus answering, said unto him, seest thou these great buildings? There shall not be left one stone upon another, that shall not be thrown down."—MARK, chap. xiii. verse 2.

AFTER THE BIRTH OF CHRIST, 31 YEARS.

JERUSALEM had sinned, and a heavy doom impended over the guilty city. The Saviour knew how forgetful of God the ungrateful Jews had been, and he also knew that it must be severely visited by Almighty wrath.

He looked on the proud structures, which seem to have moved the admiration of his disciples, and told them that all its splendour would soon be no more.

Sitting on the Mount of Olives, over against the temple, he gazed in solemn meditation on the scene before him, and then instructed his disciples what should be seen in future days.

Peter, John, James, and Andrew, were with him, and he warned them, that impostors would appear and declare that they were the promised Messiah. Further, he announced to them, that there would be "wars and rumours of wars;" that "kingdom should rise up against kingdom, and nation against nation;" that there should be "earthquakes in divers places," and there shall be famine and trouble, "but the end," he added, "shall not be yet."

These were awfully-startling prophecies, but who shall say they have not been fulfilled? Artful men and madmen have, at different periods, endeavoured to impose upon mankind, by impiously pretending that they were sent to save the world, each declaring himself to be the Son of God; thus sinning against truth, and seeking to dishonour Christ.

Wars have raged, earthquakes have been witnessed, famines and troubles have been deplored, but "the end is not yet." These dread events ought to be borne in mind. Religion calls on reason to listen to their admonishing voice. They verify what was foretold, and should warn both old and young, how dreadful are the visitations sent by an outraged Deity, that they may not neglect those observances which Scripture teaches will recommend them to his mercy and his love.

PRECIOUS OINTMENT POURED ON THE HEAD OF CHRIST

# PRECIOUS OINTMENT POURED ON THE HEAD OF CHRIST.

"And being in Bethany in the house of Simon the leper, as he sat at meat, there came a woman having an alabaster box of ointment of spikenard very precious; and she brake the box, and poured it on his head."—MARK, chap. xiv., verse 3.

AFTER THE BIRTH OF CHRIST 33 YEARS.

WHILE the chief priests and others sought to compass the destruction of the Saviour, a female in Bethany, moved by pity for his danger, or by admiration of his goodness, or probably by both, came and poured some precious ointment on his head.

Upon seeing this, some of those who were about him, remarked indignantly on the waste, so they termed it, thus committed, remarking, that "it might have been sold for more than three hundred pence, and have been given to the poor," and they murmured against the woman for what she had done.

"Then," said Jesus, "Let her alone; why trouble ye her? She hath wrought a good work on me. For ye have the poor with you always, and whensoever ye will, ye may do them good: but me ye have not always. She has done

## PRECIOUS OINTMENT POURED ON CHRIST'S HEAD.

what she could; she is come aforehand to anoint my body to the burying."

If, for a moment, we pause to reflect how great, how glorious, how good, and withal how mournfully distressed the Saviour was at that period, oh! who would think that any ointment, however precious, would be wasted if poured on that august and sacred head!

"Verily, I say unto you," Christ then said, " wheresoever this gospel shall be preached throughout the whole world, this also, that she hath done, shall be spoken of for a memorial of her."

And true the Saviour's words have proved. More than eighteen hundred years have passed since the incident, and still the kindly feeling this woman evinced almost in the last sad hours of the Saviour's mortal existence, when she anointed him for the grave, is remembered and honoured in every Christian land. No wealth could have purchased fame like that which has rewarded her reverential tenderness.

JESUS FINDS THE DISCIPLES SLEEPING

# JESUS FINDS THE DISCIPLES SLEEPING.

"And he cometh, and findeth them sleeping, and saith unto Peter, Simon, sleepest thou? couldest not thou watch one hour? Watch ye and pray lest ye enter into temptation."
—MARK, chap. xiv., verses 37, 38.

AFTER THE BIRTH OF CHRIST, 33 YEARS.

DEEPLY affecting is the narrative which St. Mark gives of the last moments of the Saviour. Those moments were sad indeed; nor can we wonder the afflicted Redeemer should desire, if it might be, that the approaching dread infliction might be spared.

Every thing that could disturb his mind was supplied by the painful circumstances which surrounded him. He knew that his blood was to be shed, that he was pursued by unrelenting enemies, and surrounded by treacherous or by timid, faint-hearted friends. By one he was about to be betrayed, by a second he was to be denied, and others were not so concerned for their Divine preceptor, but in his hour of bitter agony they could compose themselves to sleep.

Peter, James, and John had accompanied him to the garden named Gethsemane. Jesus directed them to sit there, and watch while he

## JESUS FINDS THE DISCIPLES SLEEPING.

prayed. Had they duly attended to him, and given notice of the approach of those who sought his life, the sacrifice might at least have been delayed.

He went forward a little, and prayed "that if it were possible the hour might pass from him," but still wishing that God's will should be done; when turning to his disciples, he found them asleep. To Peter he addressed these mild but cutting questions. "Simon, sleepest thou? Couldest not thou watch one hour?" He added—"Watch ye and pray, lest ye enter into temptation. The spirit truly is ready, but the flesh is weak."

Still negligent of duty, a second and a third time the doomed Jesus found the disciples sleeping. This sorely tried his patience, and provoked the mournful reproach, "Sleep on now, and take *your* rest, for the son of man is betrayed." Immediately afterwards, the armed men brought to the garden by Judas, "laid their hands on him and took him."

Young hearts, awake to feeling, and true to nature, must compassionate the Saviour, and blame the sleepy disciples; let them see that they keep awake, "and watch and pray, lest they enter into temptation."

JESUS BROUGHT BEFORE THE HIGH PRIEST.

## JESUS TAKEN BEFORE THE HIGH PRIEST.

"And they led Jesus away to the high priest: and with him were assembled all the chief priests, and the elders, and the scribes."—MARK, chap. xiv., verse 53.

AFTER THE BIRTH OF CHRIST, 33 YEARS.

WHEN wretched men suffer themselves to be moved by envy, and carried away by malice, their progress in wickedness, is commonly very great. The enemies of the Saviour, astonished at the wonderful things he did, confounded by his powerful reasoning, and worse than that, shamed by his blameless conduct and unbending virtue, were more bitter against him than ever; and at length, moved by Judas, they made him a prisoner.

When Jesus found himself surrounded by men armed with swords and staves, he demanded of them if they had come out, as against a thief, to take him? Without answering, they led him away to the palace of the high priest.

The chief priest, the elders, and the scribes, were all assembled there. They sought for witnesses whose evidence might justify them

## JESUS TAKEN BEFORE THE HIGH PRIEST.

in putting Jesus to death, but they could discover none. They indeed found wicked men ready to depose against him, but, as will always happen to those who are so depraved as to tell falsehoods of an innocent person, "their witness agreed not together;"

The high priest then questioned Jesus himself, and asked "art thou the Christ, the Son of the Blessed?"

What an answer did this call forth—it was startling; it was grand; it was sublime! Christ said, "I am, and ye shall see the Son of Man sitting on the right hand of power, and coming in the clouds of Heaven."

The high priest pretended to be shocked at the wickedness of Christ. He rent his clothes, and said, "What need we any further witnesses? Ye have heard the blasphemy; what think ye?" The high priest was of course a man of great influence. All present in the council agreed with him, that Jesus had spoken blasphemy, and condemned him to death.

The worst passions of men have often been indulged, under pretence of punishing unhappy persons said to have sinned against the majesty of Heaven. He takes upon himself a fearful responsibility, who punishes that of which God alone can judge.

THEY BADE HIM PROPHESY

# THEY BADE HIM PROPHESY.

"Some began to spit on him, and to cover his face, and to buffet him, and to say unto him, Prophesy: and the servants did strike him with the palms of their hands."—MARK, chap. xiv., verse 65.

AFTER THE BIRTH OF CHRIST, 31 YEARS.

AFTER the appeal of the high priest, the decree against our Saviour was pronounced, and impious mortals prepared to deal with the blameless captive in their hands, as if he had been proved to be the greatest possible offender against Divine and human laws; the vilest of the vile.

Such had been the Saviour's whole career, that it might have been expected those who coveted his death, that a powerful reformer might be removed out of their way, would have desired that it should be accomplished as gently as possible. The opposite of this was witnessed.

No indignity was judged too monstrous to be offered to him who had been gentleness and love personified. Some began to spit on him, and to cover his face, and to buffet him, and to say unto him "Prophesy." By that they meant to invite him to prophesy what their barbarity would presently undertake; and to this startling mockery, they added the outrage of letting "the servants strike him with the palms of their hands."

Such were the wrongs endured by the Son of the Most High! Such was the mad, the shameful conduct of those he came to save!

The mighty sacrifice Christ was content to make, to effect the redemption of sinners, it will be seen was rendered so appalling, that an additional pang imagination could scarcely suggest. He was mocked with scoffing speeches, spit upon, and struck by base hands; and all this before the punishment to which he had been cruelly doomed, was considered to have commenced. The execution on the cross was horrible; but this was not all Christ had to endure. An exile from the realms of light, he had to suffer through a mortal life all the ills of poverty and scorn. Had the cup—the last bitter draught, been allowed to pass from him; had he never been crowned with thorns, nailed to the cross, or pierced with a spear, he might still have been correctly described as "a man of sorrow, acquainted with grief."

# PETER'S REPENTANCE.

"And the second time the cock crew. And Peter called to mind the word that Jesus said unto him, Before the cock crow twice, thou shalt deny me thrice. And when he thought thereon, he wept."—MARK, chap. xiv., verse 72.

AFTER THE BIRTH OF CHRIST, 33 YEARS.

IN those moments of sadness when the mighty sacrifice which Christ came to make for the immortal benefit of man, was advancing to completion, when sorrows fast accumulated on the devoted Redeemer, when many, regarding him as an impious cheat, thought no insult too gross, no outrage too cruel to be offered to the lamb destined for slaughter, Peter declared that, however the rest of mankind were affected, though all beside should join to desert or betray, he would remain faithful, and never shrink from duty. Christ knew him to be sincere, but he also knew him to be frail, and predicted with respect to the too-confident disciple, that before the cock should crow twice, he would deny his suffering master thrice.

All this took place. Peter wished to escape observation, when a female recognised him, and said, "Thou also wast with Jesus of Nazareth." That which ought to have been then, and which was afterwards, his glory, he wanted courage and magnanimity to avow. He declared that he knew not what the speaker meant. Then the cock crew. Twice afterwards, with little variation, he did the same, and falsely declared that "he knew not the man" thus pointed at by the finger of scorn.

The cock crew a second time, and the erring follower of the Lord, recalled with shame and sorrow the words which his persecuted master had addressed to him. With grief and shame he saw how mournfully he had wandered from duty, and he wept.

Bitter, most bitter, must have been his reflections at that moment. Christ had declared that those who were ashamed of him here, he would not acknowledge in his father's kingdom. The disciple felt that to escape the contempt, or it might be the cruelty of the world, he had risked the loss of heaven and everlasting happiness.

The conduct of Peter should teach the true believer to be humble. He must not be too confident in his own strength. "Let him who standeth take heed lest he fall." Peter wept, and well might he weep for his fault; but his repentance, prompt and sincere, saved him.

SIMON THE CYRENIAN
COMPELLED TO BEAR THE CROSS

# SIMON, THE CYRENIAN, COMPELLED TO BEAR THE CROSS.

"And they compel one Simon a Cyrenian, who passed by, coming out of the country, the father of Alexander and Rufus, to bear his cross."—MARK, chap. xv., verse 21.

AFTER THE BIRTH OF CHRIST, 33 YEARS.

THE youthful student, who owns the pious and sensible wish to possess himself in early life of Christian knowledge, cannot too carefully or too often turn his attention to the sufferings of the Saviour in the latter days of his earthly course. Such information is, under any circumstances, exceedingly desirable. It will teach the unfortunate submission to the will of the Eternal, in every imaginable situation. Many sufferers condemned to die have derived the sweetest consolation, from tracing in the history of Jesus

"The path he marked for us to tread
And what he's doing for us now."

His example, while persecuted by men, has given them courage, as his promises have supplied them with more than heavenly hope, with a blessed assurance that a short course of sorrow, would introduce them to eternal joy.

The narrative of St. Mark shows that when

## SIMON COMPELLED TO BEAR THE CROSS.

Christ was charged with declaring himself King of the Jews, he returned no answer. On a certain festive occasion it was customary to give liberty to one who had been imprisoned. Pilate now offered to release Jesus, or to let loose a murderer named Barabbas, who had been implicated in some recent insurrectionary movement. Pilate rashly concluded that the people generally, were not so misled, but they would prefer the blameless Nazarite being set at large, to sparing a rebel assassin the just punishment of his guilt. Their decision was contrary to what he expected, and Barabbas was allowed to go free, while Christ having first been scourged, was handed over to them to be crucified. He was in mockery clothed in purple, and a crown of thorns was placed on his sacred head. The tormentors then spit upon, smote him with a cane or reed, and this cruel sport concluded, they led him out to die.

Jesus was sinking beneath the weight of the cross, which he had been made to carry, and it was only then, when he could sustain the burden no longer, that one Simon, a Cyrenian, was compelled to undertake it.

Such were some of the indignities and pains submitted to by Christ for man's redemption.

JESUS GIVEN TO CHRIST ON THE CROSS

# VINEGAR GIVEN TO CHRIST ON THE CROSS.

"One ran and filled a spunge full of vinegar, and put it on a reed, and gave him to drink."—MARK, chap. xv., verse 36.

AFTER THE BIRTH OF CHRIST, 33 YEARS.

THE unrelenting foes of Jesus, who took him from the presence of Pilate in order to put him to death, having forced the Cyrenian to carry the instrument of punishment which the victim had not strength left to bear, soon reached Golgotha, "which is, being interpreted, the place of a skull." Here the only movement that seems to bear the impress of tenderness or pity towards the destined victim, was witnessed, and we are told "they gave him to drink wine mingled with myrrh." It is, however, added, "but he received it not."

Throughout the final scene the Jews manifested no other touch of compassion. They crucified the Lord between two thieves, and even when they saw the form of Jesus suspended from the cross, while he experienced insufferable torture, "they that passed by railed on him, wagging their heads, and saying, Ah, thou that destroyest the temple, and buildest it in three

## VINEGAR GIVEN TO CHRIST ON THE CROSS.

days, save thyself, and come down from the cross." Likewise also the chief priests mocking, said among themselves with the scribes, "He saved others, himself he cannot save."

Not all the insults they had offered, nor all the wrongs they had inflicted on the bleeding form of Jesus, seem to have exhausted the malice of his foes. "King of Israel," they cried with heartless derision, "descend now from the cross, that we may see and believe." While he was thus mocked, the sixth hour arrived, and darkness, unlooked-for darkness, came over the land, as if nature herself could no longer endure a spectacle so awful. The gloom thus thrown over the scene, continued during three hours. Christ, in the extremity of his woe exclaimed, quoting a Psalm, "My God, my God, why hast thou forsaken me!" When he had thus spoken one ran and filled a spunge with vinegar that he might drink. Even in that moment the taunting cry which had been raised before was repeated.

Death now relieved Jesus from mortal sufferings. He heard no more the wretched jeers of exulting tormentors. The sacrifice he came to make, a fearful one to contemplate, was completed.

OATH OF ARIMATHEA FOR THE BODY OF CHRIST.

# JOSEPH OF ARIMATHÆA BEGS THE BODY OF JESUS.

"Joseph of Arimathæa, an honourable counsellor, which also waited for the kingdom of God, came, and went in boldly unto Pilate, and craved the body of Jesus."—MARK, chap. xv., verse 43.

AFTER THE BIRTH OF CHRIST, 33 YEARS.

THE last agonies of the Saviour of the world, were witnessed by some compassionate women, and when at length his sufferings terminated with his life, they, with a gentleness appropriate to their sex, were anxious to give the loved remains of him whom they could not save from death, funereal honours.

Moved by their distress, and perhaps by their entreaties, Joseph of Arimathæa, a good and worthy man, who we are told "waited for the kingdom of God," and doing so was, it is not hazarding much to conclude, assured of the true character of Jesus, presented himself boldly before Pilate, and craved that the remains of the sufferer might be handed over to him for interment. This application caused the governor to experience some surprise, as he supposed the tortures of Christ on the cross, had not so soon reached their close. He, how-

## JOSEPH BEGS THE BODY OF JESUS.

ever, enquired of the centurion, who was near at hand, if such were the case, and, satisfied on that point, he granted the prayer of Joseph.

This favour obtained, the latter did all that kindness and veneration could suggest in honour of the dead. He caused the body to be wrapped in fine linen, surrounded it with costly new spices, and then had it deposited in his own new tomb, and placed a great stone over the mouth thereof.

The anxious care of Joseph that the rites of sepulture should be duly attended to, in the case of the Saviour, proves that he knew how to admire the excellence of his conduct while he deigned to sojourn among the sons of men. We cannot but wonder that any one should have failed to do so.

It should be the anxious desire of those who read this, to guard against copying the sad error of the Jews in regard to the Redeemer. Let them covet in all things so far as in them lies, to honour him. Joseph seeing but a ghastly unconscious corpse, desired to offer all that tender sympathy could supply. What then ought Christians to feel who know that he has risen again, and know that in all their sorrows they may look to him for succour! He can save them, even from themselves.

AN ANGEL PROCLAIMS THE RESURRECTION OF JESUS.

# AN ANGEL PROCLAIMS THE RESURRECTION OF JESUS.

"He saith unto them, Be not affrighted: Ye seek Jesus of Nazareth, which was crucified: he is not here: behold the place where they laid him."—MARK, chap. xvi., verse 6.

AFTER THE BIRTH OF CHRIST, 33 YEARS.

AFFECTION loves to visit the tomb which has received the mortal remains of those we loved in life. The two Marys, now that Jesus was consigned to the grave, took sweet spices to anoint him. They wanted strength to remove the stone which covered the mouth of the sepulchre, "and who," they in sadness exclaimed, "shall roll away the stone?"

But their pious care was soon at an end. They looked and they saw that the stone was already rolled away. Minds awake to the superintending goodness which watches over the path of the faithful worshipper, often find, while journeying through life, that the difficulty which they had feared would be great, almost too much for them to grapple with, has been removed by a kind Providence, without any effort being required on their part. They saw with melancholy satisfaction, that the tomb was open to them, but what must have been

## AN ANGEL PROCLAIMS CHRIST'S RESURRECTION.

their amazement to hear, how great their delight, when they were informed, by one who though presented to them in the form of a "young man clothed in white," had in his air and countenance that which told he was of celestial origin, and when they heard from angel lips, the glad sounds, that the Christ whom they mourned was no longer a tenant of the grave, but had risen to glorious everlasting life.

Theirs was a joy not selfish. In the marvellous consummation it was theirs to hail, in that important hour, the Marys might rejoice that they had indeed seen the Lord's salvation, and the salvation of all mankind. They saw that "the last enemy" had been conquered. Christ rising from the dead proved that man is born for immortality, and that those the angel of peace calls away are not lost for ever. Thenceforward their strain might be—

> "Oh! weep not for the friends that pass
>   Into the lonesome grave,
> As breezes sweep the withered grass
>   Along the restless wave;
> For though thy pleasures may depart,
>   And darksome days be given,
> And lonely though on earth thou art,
> Yet bliss awaits the holy heart,
>   When friends rejoin in heaven."

CHRIST APPEARING TO MARY

# CHRIST APPEARING TO MARY.

"Now when Jesus was risen early the first day of the week, he appeared first to Mary Magdalene, out of whom he had cast seven devils."—MARK, chap. xvi., verse 9.

AFTER THE BIRTH OF CHRIST, 33 YEARS.

IT must strike every one at first as strange that the Jews should have been so wanting to themselves as not to rejoice in the high honour conferred on them, as well as the mighty, the everlasting benefit offered to all, by the appearance of the Son of God among them. The pious and generous young mind, cannot dwell on the great event without feeling that Christ's advent ought to have given them unmixed delight, and surprise will naturally be felt that they could be so blind as not to welcome the divine visitor with transports of joy.

But the Jews of that period were under the control of their priests; and these, forgetful of the solemn duties which attached to the sacred functions they had taken upon themselves, thought more of preserving the good things of this world, which they already plentifully enjoyed, than of celebrating the approach of him who was to conduct mankind to a better. Hence they were incredulous when they were told of

## CHRIST APPEARING TO MARY.

Jesus and his miracles. They treated all the reports which reached them, notwithstanding their truth was vouched for by thousands, with scorn, and denounced them as wretched falsehoods.

They took great care to guard against the body being removed, as they feared it might be carried off by his disciples, and that by their means it might go forth that he had risen from the dead, as had been predicted. All the precautions they could use, however, proved vain. On the third day the Saviour left the sepulchre, and appeared to Mary Magdalene. She made known what she had seen, but even his disciples, after beholding him put to death, and hearing him spoken of as a deceiver, doubted the truth of her statement. They, "when they heard that he was alive, and had been seen of her, believed not." After that he appeared to two of them, but still the residue did not believe what they told.

This unbelief prevailed even among those who might have been expected to prove least accessible to doubt. Further proofs were wanting to re-establish their faith, but these were, in mercy, soon supplied.

CHRIST APPEARS TO HIS DISCIPLES

# CHRIST APPEARS TO HIS DISCIPLES.

"Afterwards he appeared unto the eleven as they sat at meat, and upbraided them with their unbelief and hardness of heart, because they believed not them which had seen him after he had risen."—MARK, chap. xvi., verse 14.

AFTER THE BIRTH OF CHRIST, 33 YEARS.

Those to whom the Saviour appeared after his crucifixion, failed not to report what they had seen, but they could not obtain credence. That the dead should rise again seemed impossible.

To put an end to all disputes on this important subject, Jesus condescended to appear to eleven of his disciples "as they sat at meat." Such an apparition must have astonished them all; but that they saw Jesus of Nazareth, who had been crucified, none of them could doubt.

He spoke to them. He reproved their unbelief and hardness of heart, as shown in their not giving credit to the relations previously made to them.

Christ then gave his disciples an important charge. "Go ye," he said, "into all the world, and preach the word to every creature. He that believeth and is baptised, shall be saved, but he that believeth not shall be

## CHRIST APPEARS TO HIS DISCIPLES.

damned." He added, "And these signs shall follow them that believe: in my name shall they cast out devils; they shall speak with new tongues; they shall take up serpents, and if they drink any deadly thing it shall not hurt them; they shall lay hands on the sick, and they shall recover."

"The artifice," says D'Israeli, "practised by Rabbinical Judaism, which finally terminated in Talmudical edicts, was to treat the sacred code as prodigal of mystic secrets hidden in a phrase, or hanging on a single word, possibly on a particular letter, to be applied in a sense literal, or symbolical, or anagogical. Hence they tell us there is not even a *letter* in the law on which huge mountains are not suspended. These are the Alps on Alps of the Talmud." When Jesus told the disciples to preach his gospel to all the world, to every creature, he did not encumber them with any of this Rabbinical machinery. His word was to be communicated in all its beautiful simplicity. To teach humility and love, to instruct men in what they owed to the eternal author of their being, to teach them to do as they would be done by, and to love one another, that was the commission which, on his rising from the tomb, his disciples received from Christ.

THE ASCENSION OF CHRIST

# THE ASCENSION OF CHRIST.

"So then after the Lord had spoken unto them, he was received up into heaven, and sat on the right hand of God."—Mark, chap. xvi., verse 19.

After the Birth of Christ, 33 years.

It is painful to trace the progress of the Saviour, from its bringing before us so much of the weakness and wickedness of men. But the close of his eventful story, sublimely images what he has taught us to hope for ourselves. After being reviled, smote, spit upon, and in various ways tortured, the grand result at last bursts on us with celestial brightness, and we find, having left the grave to which, by the care of Joseph of Arimathæa, he was consigned, and instructed his disciples to "preach the gospel in all the world," he was at length received into heaven, the home of his Eternal Father, and seated on the right hand of God!

The momentous revelation thus made to us, interesting in itself, is full of glorious promise to all the pious. How soothing is the thought suggested by the life of the Saviour, his sufferings, and his passage to heaven! Great as the wrongs which he received at the hands of the sons of men had been, awful as his trials were,

## THE ASCENSION OF CHRIST.

they bear no comparison to the unending bliss which, his mighty task performed, was reserved for him above the sky.

Ought not this to cheer and to sustain the humblest of his followers? Seems not a voice from above to say—" Pale sufferer in this vale of tears, sorrow presses thee down, time has blanched thine hair, so much of it as remains to thee! thine eyes are dim, thy tottering limbs can scarcely sustain thy faded form! age and poverty depress thy spirits, cruel men devour thy substance, and threaten thy life! yet still this day of affliction, thou mayest be assured, shall pass away, and the present darkness be succeeded by 'marvellous light.' The gloom of the grave leads but to heavenly glory, and thou, in the presence of him who hast redeemed thee, shalt rise superior to the world and all its scorn, its griefs and afflictions, to know blessed repose in 'the bosom of thy father and thy God.'"

THE ANGEL APPEARING TO ZACHARIAS

# THE ANGEL APPEARING TO ZACHARIAS.

"And there appeared unto him an angel of the Lord, standing on the right side of the altar of incense."—LUKE, chap. i., verse 11.

---

ZACHARIAS, a priest, who lived in the time of Herod, king of Judea, had a wife of the race of Aaron. They were both righteous people before God, observing his ordinances, and of blameless life. They had been married many years, and had no child; and becoming old they expected no offspring.

One day Zacharias went to the temple to offer incense. A multitude of people were there, praying, when suddenly an angel from heaven appeared on the right side of the altar. The priest saw the glorious stranger, and dread came over him, but he was soon comforted, as the angel called to him not to fear, for the prayer which he in former days had addressed to the Most High, was heard, and long as he had waited in vain it would still be granted. His wife Elisabeth would give birth to a son, and call him John. "He," it was added by the heavenly messenger, "should be a source of joy and gladness, and many would rejoice in

## THE ANGEL APPEARING TO ZACHARIAS.

his birth," for "great in the sight of the Lord," and "filled with the Holy Ghost," he should cause many to turn to the Lord their God.

Other blessed effects, it was added, should result from his ministry. The astonished Zacharias could hardly believe what he heard, though it came from the lips of an angel.

His doubts were soon removed. "I," said the stranger, "am the angel Gabriel, who stands in the presence of God, and am sent to announce the glad tidings."

He added, Zacharias should from that time remain dumb, because he had doubted, till what was announced came to pass.

When Zacharias went forth he was speechless. The people looked on him with amazement, but dumb he remained till his wife, Elisabeth, became a mother.

The child, according to the command, was called John, since known in the religious world as John the Baptist.

Nothing is impossible to the Almighty. Prayer, though it may not be immediately answered, if offered in the spirit of true devotion, will procure blessings from above, for which weak mortals, wanting faith, could not presume to hope.

THE ANGEL APPEARING TO THE VIRGIN MARY

# THE ANGEL APPEARING TO THE VIRGIN MARY.

"The angel Gabriel was sent from God unto a city of Galilee named Nazareth, to a virgin espoused to a man whose name was Joseph, of the house of David, and the virgin's name was Mary."—LUKE, chap. i., verses 26, 27.

---

GREAT and extraordinary was the announcement of the birth of John the Baptist, but something still more extraordinary, still more glorious was to follow. The angel Gabriel came again to earth, and appeared to the Virgin Mary, the youthful wife of a man named Joseph, who dwelt in Nazareth, a city of Galilee. He came and addressed her thus: "Hail, thou that art highly favoured, the Lord is with thee: blessed art thou among women."

A mortal being cannot gaze on immortality without awe. Gracious as the speech of the angel was, it caused Mary to experience infinite alarm. He however went on to declare that she had found favour with God, and should become the mother of a son who should be named Jesus, and called "the Son of the Highest." He added, "and the Lord God shall give unto him the throne of his father David: and he shall reign over the house of

## THE ANGEL APPEARING TO THE VIRGIN MARY.

Jacob for ever; and of his kingdom there shall be no end."

Mary, wondering at what she heard, was at a loss to imagine how these things could be brought about, when she was informed that "the power of the Highest" would overshadow her, and that the infant to which she was to give birth must be called the Son of God.

Further, the angel mentioned that her cousin Elisabeth, who had long been childless, would bear a son. "For," said he, "with God nothing shall be impossible."

Mary, after this important revelation, could no longer doubt. What her feelings must have been at finding a lot so distinguished was reserved for her, no language can tell. She received the tidings with pious joy, and submissively replied to the angel, "Behold the handmaid of the Lord; be it unto me according to thy word."

When Mary had thus intimated her gratitude and her hope, the angel departed from her.

In her case, as in that of Elisabeth, we see the will and over-ruling power of the Eternal can be governed by no circumstances that ordinarily regulate the fortunes of men.

ELIZABETH VISITED BY MARY.

# ELISABETH VISITED BY MARY.

"Mary arose in those days, and went into the hill country with haste, into a city of Juda; and entered into the house of Zacharias and saluted Elisabeth."—LUKE, chap. i., verses 39, 40.

AFTER the astonishing revelation made to the Virgin Mary by the angel Gabriel, she visited Elisabeth. She was probably moved to do this, in consequence of learning from the speech of her celestial visitor that her cousin was also largely favoured by the Almighty, though not to the same extent as herself.

If any doubt lingered on her mind, in regard to that which at first seemed so hard of belief, it must have been dismissed when she saw Elisabeth, for the latter no sooner heard her salutation, than she felt like one inspired in an extraordinary degree, and in the language of the Evangelist, "she was filled with the Holy Ghost," and with an air of joyous congratulation, using the exact words of the angel, "she spake out with a loud voice, and said, Blessed art thou among women."

Elisabeth then exulted in the honour conferred upon her by Mary; seeing, as she expressed herself, "that the mother of her Lord should come to her."

## ELISABETH VISITED BY MARY.

She indulged in other reflections of the like gratifying character. "My soul," she exclaimed, "doth magnify the Lord, my spirit hath rejoiced in God my Saviour."

"For he," she added, "hath regarded the low estate of his handmaiden, for behold from henceforth all generations shall call me blessed."

We see here that Mary had a distinct view of the honour in which her name would be held in all time to come. She rejoiced in the great things that "he that is mighty" had done to her; she rejoiced in knowing that he had "scattered the proud in the imagination of their hearts," had "put down the mighty from their seats, and exalted them of low degree," while he had "filled the hungry with good things and sent the rich empty away."

Occupied with these heavenly musings, we see the mercy and the goodness of God, filled Mary with pious and delightful anticipations, and made her truly "Blessed among women."

THE INFANT ST. JOHN.

# THE INFANT ST. JOHN.

"The child grew, and waxed strong in spirit, and was in the deserts till the day of his shewing unto Israel."—LUKE, chap. i., verse 80.

AFTER THE BIRTH OF CHRIST. 4 YEARS.

The Virgin Mary remained with her cousin Elisabeth, during three months, and till she brought forth a son.

Thus was fulfilled the prophecy or announcement made by the angel Gabriel to Zacharias and Elisabeth. When the time to name the child arrived, it was proposed that he should be called "Zacharias, after the name of his father." To that his mother opposed herself, and said, "he shall be called John."

Her speaking thus, caused some surprise to be expressed by friends about her. It was customary in that country, as it is now in England, to give an infant the name of his father or of some near relation, and it was remarked to Elisabeth, that none of her kindred were known by the name which she wished her child to bear. Indeed considerable resistance was offered to her wish, and signs were made to Zacharias, that he might decide the question which had been raised.

## THE INFANT ST. JOHN.

The aged priest, it will be remembered, was bereft of speech from the time when the angel appeared to him. He now signified that he wished a writing-table to be brought to him, which being done, he wrote on it, "His name is John."

This caused surprise to those who stood by, but greater amazement still was witnessed, when on a sudden, he, who had so many months been dumb, suddenly found his "tongue loosed."

The priest Zacharias made use of the organ so miraculously withdrawn, and so happily restored, by praising God. He raised his voice and cried, "Blessed be the Lord God of Israel, for he hath visited and redeemed his people." He rejoiced in the promised mercy of the Lord, while with more than the fondness of a father, even with the prescience of a holy prophet, he pronounced that John should "go before the face of the Lord, to prepare his ways; to give light to them that sit in darkness and in the shadow of death, and to guide our feet into the way of peace."

Such were the expectations raised and speedily fulfilled in the case of the infant St. John.

THE NATIVITY

## THE NATIVITY.

" And she brought forth her first-born son, and wrapped him in swaddling-clothes, and laid him in a manger; because there was no room for them in the inn."—LUKE, chap. ii., verse 7.

THAT great event in the history of the world, the birth of Jesus Christ, as recorded by St. Luke, is brought before us in so familiar a style, that it has about it all the freshness of a contemporary report. No grandeur of language is affected. The advent of the Redeemer required no factitious aid to make its vast importance understood, by countless generations of men.

The narrative is as simple and as unostentatious as the mortal parents of Jesus were; as simple as the means at their command, when Christ was born; when the infant, having been wrapped in swaddling clothes, was laid in a manger. The Son of the Almighty was thus disposed of, "because there was no room for Joseph and Mary in the inn." When it is stated that "there was no room *for them*," we may conclude that if they had been persons of higher degree, that is of greater importance, in a worldly point of view, a more fitting place might have been found for the mother and her child.

## THE NATIVITY.

It happened at the time, when Christ was born, that there were in the same country shepherds abiding in the field, keeping watch over their flock by night. "To them the angel of the Lord appeared, and the glory of the Lord shone round about them." That which had taken place on earth, was at that moment the subject of a grand celebration in Heaven. To the Heavenly host it was known that Christ thus commenced his important mission. Their pure intelligence was not blind to the greatness of the undertaking. But ambition of higher glory, of accomplishing more that is great and good, we may hence conclude is not unknown in Heaven. The angels who "stand before the throne" knew that Christ's object was mercy, and they knew that he who took upon himself the difficult, the painful labour of seeking it, was equal to the task, and that in performing it, while saving sinners, he would exalt his own name through all eternity.

# ANGELS PROCLAIM THE BIRTH OF CHRIST.

"And the angel said unto them, Fear not, for behold I bring you good tidings of great joy, which shall be to all people."—LUKE, chap. ii., verse 10.

It will easily be conceived that the insufferable splendour of an inhabitant of the sky cannot be looked upon by mortal eyes without fear. The shepherds, when they saw the angel, were affrighted. He marked their alarm, and hastened to dissipate it by saying, "Fear not; for behold I bring you good tidings, of great joy, which shall be to all people. For unto you is born this day in the city of David, a Saviour, which is Christ the Lord."

Having briefly imparted what had taken place, he mentioned some of the circumstances connected with the birth of Jesus. "This," he said, shall be a sign unto you; ye shall find the babe wrapped in swaddling clothes, lying in a manger."

Possessed of such intelligence, the favoured shepherds were permitted to witness on earth that worthy commemoration which had already commenced in Heaven. The celestial brethren of the angel descended from the sky, and joined company with the speaker, to proclaim the goodness of the Omnipotent; for we read, "And suddenly there was with the angel a multitude of the Heavenly host, praising God, and saying, Glory to God in the highest, and on earth peace and good-will towards men."

The boldest flights of poetry have imaged nothing more magnificent than this scene. What could surpass in grandeur the descent of a multitude of seraphim and cherubim from the opening sky! Had anything been wanting, it would have been supplied by the sublime theme which united their voices, while they sung, "Glory to God, peace on earth, and good-will to men."

Thus distinctly was it announced that Christ took upon himself a mortal form, to promote peace and good-will; thus clearly was it intimated to those who claim to be numbered among his followers, that it is their duty, as it was his high mission, to extend the reign of peace, and to dispose men to love one another.

Reassured by what they had heard, the shepherds soon threw off their fear, and prepared to journey to Bethlehem, to see with their own eyes what the Lord by his angels had made known to them.

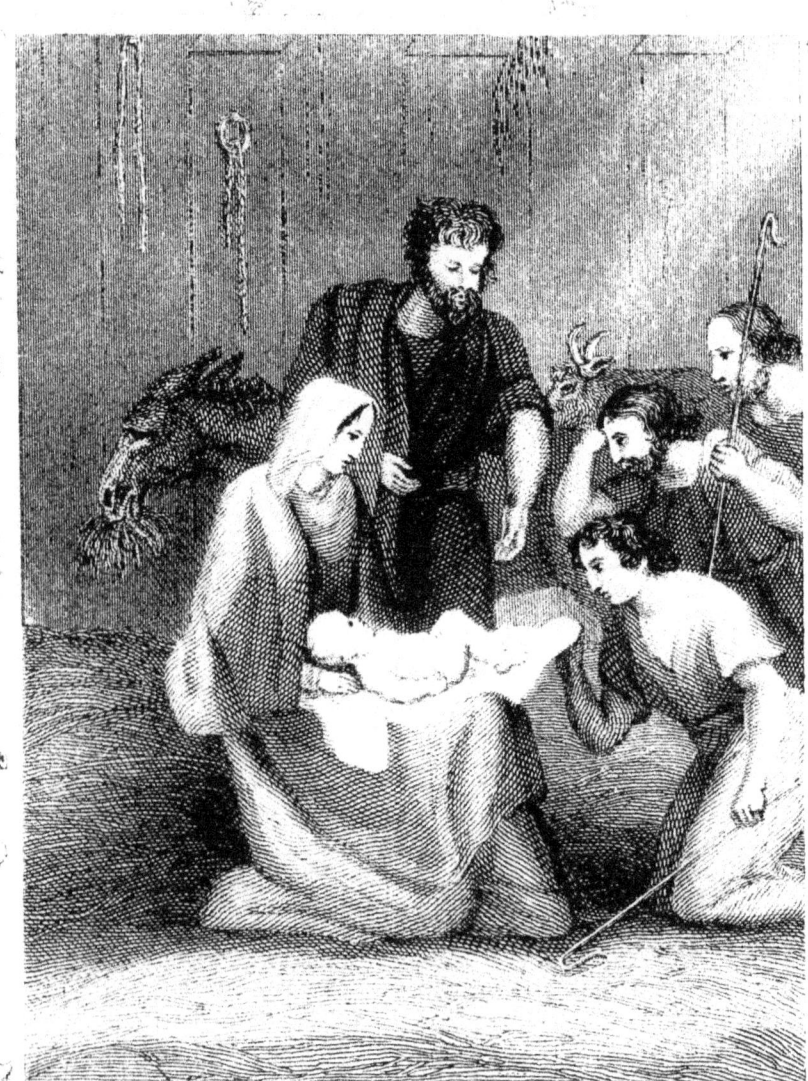

ADORATION OF THE SHEPHERDS

# ADORATION OF THE SHEPHERDS.

"And they came with haste, and found Mary, and Joseph, and the babe lying in a manger."—LUKE, chap. ii., verse 16.

LITTLE could the shepherds, when they on that memorable night which witnessed the birth of the Lord, went forth to watch their flocks, have expected to hear of such an event; little could they have expected to see a multitude of angels, and hear the Heavenly chorus which burst on their astonished senses. Having listened to the celestial strain, and been told by what signs they might know the infant, whose coming had been thus announced, they lost no time in journeying to Bethlehem, and appear to have had no difficulty in finding the objects of their search. They found Mary and Joseph lodged in a stable, and the babe lying in a manger. What they saw, and what had been so miraculously made known to them, they reported abroad. The glad tidings were received with wonder. Mary rejoiced, in the belief that the promised Messiah had come, and the shepherds having had the fullest confirmation of that which had been communicated by the

## ADORATION OF THE SHEPHERDS.

Heavenly messenger, returned glorifying and praising God for all that they had heard.

In the humble guise, above described, the Son of God was first presented to mortal view. Was it to teach all who in future times might desire to honour his name, that lowliness in this world is not to be despised. To that infant, seen by the shepherds lying in a manger, the hopes of all Christians have for many ages turned. In all circumstances, in him they seek a friend and comforter. "But," says the pious Hervey, "especially when the hour of thy departure approaches, when 'thy flesh and thy heart fail,' when all the springs of life are irreparably breaking, then look unto Jesus with a believing eye. Like expiring Stephen, behold him standing at the right hand of God, on purpose to succour his people in their last extremity. O then," adds the same admired writer, "be sure to look to Jesus! See by faith the Lord's Christ; view him as the only way to the everlasting mansion, as the only door to the abodes of bliss."

THE NAMING OF JESUS.

# THE NAMING OF JESUS.

"When eight days were accomplished, his name was called Jesus, which was so named of the angel."—LUKE, chap. ii., verse 21.

---

THE Jews had various rites in common usage, which need not here be minutely detailed. One of their customs which seems rarely to have been neglected, was to name their children when they were eight days old.

This was done in the case of the infant Jesus. "When eight days were accomplished," he was so called, according to the Jewish forms. In his case, like that of St. John, the name had been dictated by a messenger from above.

In early times the distinguishing appellations given to men or children had reference to the offices which they were expected to fill, or the duties they were to undertake. The word Jesus, means Saviour, and Christ has, in the Greek tongue, the same signification as Messiah in the Hebrew language, and is equivalent to *anointed*, or *ordered* to fill an office.

That he was so ordered or appointed we have from his own mouth. In the gospel of St. John, when praying to his Eternal Father, he describes himself to have been *sent* to make men know "the only true God and Jesus

## THE NAMING OF JESUS.

Christ." Further, he says, "I have glorified thee on the earth, I have finished the work which thou *gavest me to do*."

Still more distinctly is this set forth in the following verse:—"And now, O Father, glorify thou me with thine own self, with the glory which I had with thee before the world was."

Thus we learn that before the creation of the world, the Saviour shared the glory of the Almighty in Heaven. Subsequently, in consequence of the heavy penalty incurred by sinful man, an important *work was given* to him. To him, in mercy to a sinful world was confided that mission, in the fulfilment of which he appeared as a mortal, suffered as a mortal, and finally died as a mortal.

Therefore as it was the object of his coming and sacrifice to save, it was ordered that he should bear the name of Jesus, or the Saviour.

THE HOLY FAMILY

# THE HOLY FAMILY.

"And the child grew, and waxed strong in spirit, filled with wisdom: and the grace of God was upon him."—LUKE, chap. ii., verse 40.

AFTER THE BIRTH OF CHRIST, 2 YEARS.

WHEN, to save man by his mediation and self-sacrifice, from the consequences of his fearful transgressions, the Son of the Almighty condescended to become a mortal, he took the form of a common child, and not only assumed it for a moment, but subjected himself to the slow progress of human growth. He not only taught and suffered as a man, but he was subjected to all the pains of infancy. With them, of course, he knew its joys; and in the beautiful group which Raphael has produced, he has given us a glimpse of the Saviour in his happiest moments. We can hardly help lamenting that they were so few; but we may be permitted to rejoice that if, in after-life, his woes were great, the glory which these gained for him is greater, and is eternal.

The artist presents him to us clasped to the bosom of his virgin mother, who experiences no common happiness at finding herself the worldly parent of the Son of the Creator of the world.

## THE HOLY FAMILY.

With fond delight she exults in the important charge confided to her, while the infant clings, with natural love, to such a mother—with that love that children, who are blessed with kind parents, ought to feel from the moment they are capable of reflection, till that in which they, by the common lot of mortality, pass to the grave.

A witness of the affectionate delight which both evidently feel—John the Baptist appears a gratified, admiring, though youthful spectator. To him it might be given, even at that early period, to contemplate the important labours which Jesus was, in the fulness of time, to accomplish. He might anticipate the great task which he himself had to perform, in preparing the way for the illustrious Redeemer.

Many passages in the history of Jesus and John serve to show, that even in early youth a knowledge of divine truth may be gained. How happy are they who wake to reflection in the spring-time of life, and who, instead of wasting their hours in idle sports and frivolous amusements, learn, from a careful perusal of the sacred page, to aspire to higher enjoyments.

CHRIST DISPUTING WITH THE DOCTORS.

# CHRIST DISPUTING WITH THE DOCTORS.

"And it came to pass, that after three days they found him in the temple, sitting in the midst of the doctors, both hearing them and asking them questions."—LUKE, chap. ii., verse 46.

AFTER THE BIRTH OF CHRIST, 12 YEARS.

At an early period of his earthly career, Jesus gave goodly promise of that wisdom which, at a later day, was to burst on the world with such dazzling, such unapproachable splendour.

Joseph and Mary were in the habit of going, every year, to Jerusalem, to assist at a solemn Jewish celebration—the feast of the passover. When Jesus was twelve years of age, they prepared, as usual, to go, and resolved to take him with them. They accordingly journeyed thither, and took part in the ceremonies, which, at times, were repeated. They appear to have lasted several days; and when they had concluded, Mary and her husband returned to their home, but missed the child on their way. On such occasions, great numbers resorted to Jerusalem, and travelled in company. Joseph and Mary expected to find Jesus in the crowd; and, disappointed in this, they

## CHRIST DISPUTING WITH THE DOCTORS.

concluded that he had found his way to some of their kindred and acquaintance; and in this belief, they went a day's journey in search of him, but without success.

They, no doubt, were greatly disturbed at this. Parents who suppose their children are lost, or in danger, can know no rest.

Thus it was with Joseph and Mary; and accordingly we are told by St. Luke, they retraced their steps to Jerusalem.

They sought him during three days, and at length discovered him seated in the temple, where he discoursed with learned doctors, asking questions; and, more than that, giving them such answers, that all were astonished at his understanding.

"But son," said the Virgin Mary, "why hast thou thus dealt with us? Behold, thy father and I have sought thee, sorrowing." He answered, "Wist ye not that I must be about my Father's business?"

A child must not distress his parents by absenting himself from them: but Jesus Christ, the Son of God, had sought the temple to confer with learned men, to qualify himself for the part which he had to perform; he was not negligently wasting his hours—he was "about his Father's business."

JESUS IN THE WILDERNESS.

# JESUS IN THE WILDERNESS

"And Jesus, being full of the Holy Ghost, returned from Jordan, and was led by the spirit into the wilderness."— LUKE, chap. iv., verse 1.

AFTER THE BIRTH OF CHRIST, 30 YEARS.

MEN of extraordinary piety, in ancient days, not unfrequently withdrew themselves from towns and cities to the desert. There contemplating the rugged face of nature, and denying themselves the ordinary comforts of civilized life, they were enabled, more earnestly, to muse on sacred things. Far removed from the vanities of the world, their untrammelled thoughts could freely seek to commune with the Author of their being, the Creator of the world, free from interruption; and

"Look through nature, up to nature's God."

In the bustle of cities, perplexed with the cares of business, and often unavoidably engaged in strife, the mind will occupy itself with cares which it is almost degradation for an immortal spirit to regard. Such is the weakness of our nature: all feel it; but a silent monitor within, in his "still small voice," fails not to whisper, "This is wrong. Oh, man! a higher destiny is yours; and is it

## JESUS IN THE WILDERNESS.

for you, alike forgetful of the purposes of your own individual being, and of that immortality which is reserved for those who are faithful to duty, thus to suffer your thoughts to dwell on objects which will eventually be found as valueless as the trifling toys which beguiled the days of infancy!"

It is in solitude that our thoughts often take a higher, nobler flight, than they can accomplish surrounded by the cares, or even the comforts of life. If the feeble voice cannot reach mortal ears at but a short distance, we feel that there is no obstacle to the slightest whisper we can breathe, gaining instant access to an Omnipresent Deity.

That consoling reflection has supported many a wanderer in a foreign land. Cut off from social intercourse with his fellows, from the solace of attending divine worship, he has still rejoiced in the blessed assurance—

"That He whose temple is all space,
Whose altar, earth, sea, skies,"

could hear the petition of the lonely one, grant what was needful for his comfort, and save him from evil. To Him let us ever be accustomed to turn our thoughts, who has promised, that when we call upon his holy name we may expect an answer.

CHRIST TEMPTED

# CHRIST TEMPTED.

"And the devil said unto him (Jesus), if thou be the Son of God, command this stone that it be made bread."—LUKE, chap. iv., verse 3.

AFTER THE BIRTH OF CHRIST, 30 YEARS.

Jesus was led by the spirit into the wilderness. The evangelist gives no intimation that it was the evil spirit that so conducted him; but while there, the devil appeared to him, and during forty days tempted him.

Fasting was one of the exercises which ancient piety most frequently used. Jesus, while tempted by Satan, refrained from food. The extraordinary situation in which he found himself, rendered him heedless of the common demands of nature, and enabled him to bear up under circumstances which otherwise would have exceeded the powers of human endurance. Eventually, he suffered from hunger.

That was the moment in which the evil one, believing him, with the wants, to have the weakness of humanity, thought fit to tempt him. Pointing to a stone, he said, "If thou be the Son of God, command this stone that it be made bread."

## CHRIST TEMPTED.

Hunger could not move the Saviour to attend to the bidding of Satan. His reply was, "Man shall not live by bread alone, but by every word of God." Common sustenance is valueless in comparison with divine intelligence.

The devil afterwards was permitted to take Jesus to the top of a mountain; and there he offered to give him all the kingdoms of the world, if our Lord would worship him.

His efforts were all in vain. He could not compass his object. Christ replied, with just disdain. "Get thee behind me," he said; "for it is written, Thou shalt worship the Lord thy God, and him only shalt thou serve."

Happy are they who, from childhood upwards, remember and profit from this striking narrative. The sons of men cannot indeed be offered so large a bribe to turn from the right path, as the devil was permitted to exhibit to Jesus; but in many of the walks of life, objects of great present importance may be thrown in their way.

The devil subsequently wanted Jesus to cast himself from a pinnacle; but all his powers were exerted in vain, and finally he departed, as he continues to do, from those who steadfastly resist the sinful bribes which may be thrown in their way.

CHRIST TEACHING IN THE SYNAGOGUE

# CHRIST TEACHING IN THE SYNAGOGUE.

"And he taught in their synagogues, being glorified of all."—LUKE, chap. iv., verse 15.

AFTER THE BIRTH OF CHRIST, 30 YEARS.

THE greater works which Jesus performed must not cause us to overlook the untiring zeal with which, on other occasions, he laboured for the benefit of mankind. He was a preacher; and, in Galilee, had obtained much fame. He taught in the synagogue, and, we may conclude, with immense success; as St. Luke tells, "He was glorified of all."

When at Nazareth, as was his custom, he went into the synagogue on the Sabbath-day, and stood up to read. The narrative proceeds—"And there was delivered unto him the book of the prophet Esaias. And when he had opened the book, he found the place where it is written, The spirit of the Lord is upon me, because he hath anointed me to preach the gospel to the poor; he hath sent me to heal the broken-hearted, to preach deliverance to the captives, and recovering of sight to the blind; to set at liberty those

## CHRIST TEACHING IN THE SYNAGOGUE.

that are bruised: to preach the acceptable year of the Lord."

In thus directing attention to the language of Esaias, he made known what was his own high mission. The envoy of God's mercy, the minister of peace, he came especially to bring gospel comfort to the poor. He was sent by his Almighty father to heal the broken-hearted.

Can any one read this unmoved? What hope must it not impart to every mourner to know that the great Creator sent his Son to this world, to relieve sinful men from the greatest evils that can press upon their imperfect nature; and, more than that, to prepare them for a happier state of being.

How comprehensive is Divine benevolence! All our wants are known to Him who made us; and though we are so far left to ourselves, that serious evils may overtake us—if we forget not our duty—if we "remember the promises," we may rest satisfied that we shall not be wholly forsaken—left to pine in hopeless sorrow, and perish in despair. Mercy provided for his spiritual necessities by giving to the world a glorious teacher, rich in wisdom, in holiness, and love.

CHRIST THE COMFORTER.

# CHRIST THE COMFORTER.

"And he began to say unto them, this day is the scripture fulfilled in your ears. And all bare him witness, and wondered at the gracious words which proceeded out of his mouth."—LUKE, chap. iv., verses 21, 22.

AFTER THE BIRTH OF CHRIST, 30 YEARS.

It has been seen, that Jesus Christ loved to refer to the prophets of Israel, and especially to dwell on passages which told the chosen people that those eminent persons, sent among them by the God of their fathers, should relieve hearts that groaned beneath incurable sorrow, and set the captive free. In his words, as in his actions, it was his aim to succour the afflicted, and to awaken hope in the desponding. Thus in all his progress, even to that dreadful moment when, raised between heaven and earth, his bleeding, mangled form hung on the cross at Calvary, he was constantly employed. Whatever his own cares, we still find him soothing the distress of others, that all might recognise in him, "Christ the comforter."

When Jesus had taught in the synagogue, as shown in former pages, "He closed the book, and gave it again to the minister, and sat down." He ceased; but the impression which he had made on his hearers was such, that they could not immediately withdraw their attention from him; for we are told, in a subsequent verse, "They were astonished at his doctrine; for his word was with power."

Nor can we much wonder at their amazement. Born of humble parents, having many difficulties to contend with in his early youth, and few of the advantages of common education; being thus seen of men, when that soul-awakening eloquence which dwelt on the Redeemer's tongue, sounded in their ears, they might well feel astonished at his bold, convincing exposition of the Scripture; while they said, one to another, "Is not this Joseph's son?"

Well might they ask such a question, when they heard the son of a poor carpenter teach them lessons of surpassing importance, and perform a task to which their most learned sages were not equal. From the humblest of mankind God has often raised up his noblest instruments of mercy; but none like his Son, Jesus Christ.

CHRIST HEALING THE SICK

# CHRIST HEALING THE SICK.

"Now when the sun was setting, all they that had any sick with divers diseases brought them unto him, and he laid his hands on every one of them, and healed them."—LUKE, chap iv., verse 40.

AFTER THE BIRTH OF CHRIST, 30 YEARS.

THE power and the goodness of the Redeemer were rendered most conspicuous by the comfort he diffused among those who were afflicted. Hunger was appeased by his kindness; the voice of mourning was checked by his presence; and sickness fled from him.

His skill in the healing art, or rather the authority vested in him, which transcended all skill, had wrought such wonders, that in the countries which he traversed, he had great fame. Fortified by priests and scoffers against the truths of religion, which he applied himself to implant in their hearts, though they might dissent from his doctrine, his ability to relieve sickness they could not deny, or even treat as a matter which was doubtful.

Accordingly we find that however men in health might neglect his teachings, when they or their friends were attacked by any fatal malady, they failed not to turn to Jesus. In

## CHRIST HEALING THE SICK.

Capernaum he had cast out devils; from the mother of Simon's wife he had dismissed a dangerous fever; and these things being known, while still he remained in that place, "when day was about to close," St. Luke tells, "that all they that had any sick brought them to him."

Nor did they seek him in vain. Ever ready to relieve the afflicted, "he laid his hands on every one of them, and healed them all."

In this we see the amazing goodness of the Saviour of man. He did not confine his kindness to those who were known to him, who had served him, or who were his devoted followers, but he restored every one of the applicants to health.

The comprehensive love thus displayed, justifies a hope that even those who are least enlightened, may yet be benefited by his mercy. It proves the excellence of the advice given by an admired Puritan writer, "Make but choice of this friend, and you shall never say of him, He is dead, I have lost him."

He who can heal the body, who could thus largely dispense his bounty to those who suffered from the diseases incident to this life, will not fail those who trust in him, to lead them to a better, and to give them that "peace which passeth all understanding."

THE MIRACULOUS DRAUGHT OF FISHES

# THE MIRACULOUS DRAUGHT OF FISHES.

"And when they had thus done, they enclosed a great multitude of fishes, and their net brake."—LUKE, chap. v., verse 6.

AFTER THE BIRTH OF CHRIST, 30 YEARS.

THE life of a fisherman is one of severe hazard and toil. He has to brave storms and all varieties of weather, and often his greatest exertions prove of little avail, and his labour is left unrewarded. In ancient times it was more perilous than it is now. The disciples, who were fishermen, in common with all who ploughed the sea, were in the habit of keeping near the shore for safety. Experience has taught men that on the wide ocean, there is more security far from land.

Christ knew this, and after teaching the people who thronged to hear him, he said to Simon, in whose vessel he found himself, to "launch out into the deep, and let down your nets for a draught."

Simon therefore replied, "Master, we have toiled the night, and have taken nothing. Nevertheless," he added, "at thy word I will let down the net."

## THE MIRACULOUS DRAUGHT OF FISHES.

Good cause had he to rejoice that he attended to the word of Jesus, for having again thrown in the net "they enclosed a multitude of fishes." The number taken was so great that the net or nets began to break, and Simon and those who were with him found it necessary to beckon to their partners, who were in another ship, to help them. They came, and caught such vast numbers of fishes that they filled both their ships enormously, till they seemed in danger of sinking.

For such a result they were not prepared, Simon Peter, when he saw it, was frightened, and "he fell at Jesus's knees, saying—Depart from me, for I am a sinful man, O Lord!"

All were astonished, but Christ soothed them, and promised that thenceforth, it should be their business " to catch men."

The miraculous draught of fishes not only relieved the present wants of Simon and his companions, but it immediately led to their gaining a higher occupation, beneficial not only to themselves, but to millions then unborn.

CHRIST HEALING THE CENTURION'S SERVANT

# CHRIST HEALING THE CENTURION'S SERVANT.

"And a certain centurion's servant who was dear unto him, was sick, and ready to die. And when he heard of Jesus, he sent unto him the elders of the Jews, beseeching him that he would come and heal his servant."—LUKE, chap. vii., verses 2, 3.

AFTER THE BIRTH OF CHRIST, 30 YEARS.

IF there is a sameness in the narratives handed down to us of the doings of the Saviour, it should always be gratefully remembered that this mainly arises from the many acts of kindness and mercy which marked his earthly career, and which he was never weary of repeating.

When Jesus had entered Capernaum, the servant of a Roman officer, a centurion, was sick and about to die. This servant was greatly valued by her master; she is said to have been "dear unto him," and when he heard of Jesus, who had effected various important cures, he sent to him and prayed that he would heal the afflicted one.

The prayer was supported by elders of the Jews, who importuned the Saviour to comply with the centurion's wish, as he was a friend

## CHRIST HEALING THE CENTURION'S SERVANT.

to the Jewish nation, and had built for them a synagogue.

Christ soon consented to go to the house in which the sick person lay. It was not very distant, but before he could approach it the anxious centurion sent other friends to him, who in effect said, "The centurion wishes you not to trouble yourself to walk to his home. He is unworthy of that honour, he is unworthy to stand in your presence. All he dare ask is that you will say the word, and confident he is that his servant will immediately be healed."

The full conviction thus manifested in the power of Jesus met with its reward. Turning to those who were near him the Redeemer said, "I have not found so great faith, no not in Israel."

He willed it and it was done. Those that had been sent to him, returning to the centurion's house, found the servant completely restored.

It was the lively faith, combined with the unaffected humility of the suppliant, which in this case prevailed. Those who first duly humble themselves, and whose confidence in the goodness of the Lord is steadfast and undoubting, will not appeal to his mercy in vain.

CHRIST RAISING THE WIDOW'S SON

# CHRIST RAISING THE WIDOW'S SON.

" Now when he came nigh to the gate of the city, behold, there was a dead man carried out, the only son of his mother, and she was a widow; and much people of the city was with her."—LUKE, chap. vii., verse 12.

AFTER THE BIRTH OF CHRIST, 30 YEARS.

IF there is anything connected with humanity pure and unalloyed by a touch of worldly feeling, it is the warm affection of a mother; if there be anything in mortal grief (brief as we know it must be) that can command reverence and sympathy, it is the woe of a mother who mourns the loss of her child. The climax is supplied when that child is an only one, and the mourner a widow.

It happened that when Jesus was approaching the gate of a city called Nain, he saw a crowd which accompanied or followed the corpse of a young man, the only son of his widowed mother.

He saw the bereft parent, and was affected at marking her distress. The tears of a woman fail not to make a deep impression on the heart of man. In this case so deeply did Christ feel

## CHRIST RAISING THE WIDOW'S SON.

for the affliction of the mourner, that he interrupted the ordinary course of nature to give her comfort.

"Weep not," said he to the disconsolate parent. Then he touched the bier on which the body was stretched. The bearers stood still, when, addressing the lifeless form, the Lord pronounced the words, "Young man, I say unto thee arise."

How must the attendant crowd have been astonished when the next moment they saw the dead man sit up; "and begin to speak." Not only did he do this, but it was soon evident that he was completely restored, and Christ delivered him to his mother.

This miracle created great amazement in the beholders. It proved to them all that Jesus was no common mortal; no mere pretender. "And there came a fear on all; and they glorified God, saying, that a great prophet is risen up among us, and that God hath visited his people."

The fame of the deed went through "all Judea, and throughout all the region round about." This might have been expected; and it might also have been hoped that such a convincing proof of the divinity of Jesus would have set unbelief at rest for ever.

THE WOMAN ANOINTING CHRIST'S FEET

# THE WOMAN ANOINTING CHRIST'S FEET.

"And, behold, a woman in the city, who was a sinner, when she knew that Jesus sat at meat in the Pharisee's house, brought an alabaster box of ointment, and stood at his feet behind him weeping, and began to wash his feet with tears, and did wipe them with the hair of her head, and kissed his feet."—LUKE chap vii., verses 37, 38.

AFTER THE BIRTH OF CHRIST, 30 YEARS.

It has often been remarked, that during the earthly wanderings of Jesus, his sorrows were most deeply mourned; his wants most kindly attended to by woman. The tenderness of the softer sex, was where he appeared most conspicuous, as if to atone for that original weakness which "brought sin into the world," and a Redeemer to suffer for it.

Christ appears to have sojourned some time in Nain. One of the Pharisees invited him to eat with him, and Jesus accepted the invitation.

While he sat at meat in the house of the Pharisee, a woman who had not led a blameless life, knowing he was there, and admiring his goodness, presented herself before him, bringing with her an alabaster box of ointment, and

## THE WOMAN ANOINTING CHRIST'S FEET.

standing with great humility at his feet behind him. Conscious of her own unworthiness, she wept. Her tears fell on the Saviour's feet. She wiped them "with the hair of her head, and anointed them with the ointment."

The Pharisee knew the woman was not a person of good life, and said to himself, that Jesus, if he had been a prophet, would at once have penetrated her character. The Lord saw the vain man's thoughts, and hastened to point out to him that this poor woman, sinner as she was, had manifested for him more kindness, more generous regard, than he had received from the Pharisee himself, who had invited him to eat. "Thou," said he, "gavest no water for my feet." (This anciently was one of the first offers of Eastern hospitality.) "She has washed them with her tears: my head with oil thou didst not anoint, but this woman hath anointed my feet."

Such marks of kindness Jesus knew how to value. He pitied one who "had loved much." The Lord will not suffer love and kindness to remain unrewarded. To the weeping but gentle-hearted frail one he addressed the all-consoling words, "Thy sins are forgiven, go in peace."

THE PARABLE OF THE SOWER

# THE PARABLE OF THE SOWER.

"A sower went out to sow his seed; and as he sowed, some fell by the way-side; and it was trodden down, and the fowls of the air devoured it."—LUKE, chap. viii., verse 5.

AFTER THE BIRTH OF CHRIST. 30 YEARS.

THE beautiful apologues known as parables, by which it was the good pleasure of Christ to instruct his followers, have been justly regarded as a treasure by many generations of men. Such they must be considered to the end of time.

A sower Christ describes to have gone forth to sow his seed, some of which fell by the way side, and it was trodden down and devoured by the fowls. Some of it fell upon a rock and withered away for want of moisture, and some fell among thorns, and was choked. But a portion of the seed fell in good ground, and brought forth a hundred-fold.

When the disciples heard this parable, they were at a loss to guess its application till the Lord enlightened them.

By the seed he imaged the word of God. That which falls by the way side is the exhortation which is not duly attended to, through the arts of the devil: that which falls on the rock pic-

## THE PARABLE OF THE SOWER.

tures the word, which is joyfully received at first, but is soon forgotten by thoughtless hearers; while that which fell among thorns, is that which is put aside by worldly cares and pleasures.

The seed spoken of as having fallen on good ground, is the word "of God which, having found its way into a good and honest heart," there remains and brings forth good fruit with patience.

Important, most important, is the knowledge thus imparted. It warns the young and the thoughtless not to neglect holy things; it admonishes those of riper years not to welcome the truth with overstrained eagerness, and then coldly disregard it. The wealthy it solemnly cautions against permitting their interests or their pleasures to render them heedless of what is of infinitely more consequence than the grandest projects on which they can be engaged in this world.

Could the voice of reason be heard, mortals would feel their interest and their duty the same. Oh! that their eyes might be opened! Then would discord, envy, and all uncharitableness be banished, and men would live in harmony and peace here, while looking forward with blissful confidence to a happier state of being, glorious and eternal.

CHRIST CASTS OUT A LEGION OF DEVILS.

# CHRIST CASTS OUT A LEGION OF DEVILS.

"And when he went forth to land, there met him out of the city a certain man which had devils long time, and ware no clothes, neither abode in any house but in the tombs."—LUKE, chap. viii., verse 27.

AFTER THE BIRTH OF CHRIST, 30 YEARS.

JOURNEYING to the country of the Gadarenes, St. Luke has recorded that the Saviour met a certain man who had been possessed of devils for a long time. His account of this unhappy man, and of the relief afforded to him by the Saviour, will be found to confirm in every particular that given of the same miracle by St. Mark. We find him described almost in the same words, as passing his time among the tombs; not resorting to the resting-place of the departed, as a wise, reflecting man will sometimes do, to reflect on the frail tenure of human existence, and assist devotional thoughts by looking on the monuments or brief histories, which may there be preserved, of those who are no more, but thither he went a distracted howling maniac, having no object, no rational thought, either of the present or of the future.

## CHRIST CASTS OUT A LEGION OF DEVILS.

As elsewhere recorded, Jesus, on beholding the sufferer, was touched with pity, and commanded the unclean spirit, or spirits, to withdraw. He was answered by one of them, who declared his name to be Legion, as he combined many evil spirits; and Legion made for them the strange request, which has already been mentioned in the proper place, recorded by St. Mark, that they might enter a herd of swine, which Christ permitted. "Then went the devils out of the man, and entered into the swine: and the herd ran violently down a steep place into the lake, and were choked."

So marvellous a narrative cannot be read without astonishment; but it will be found that more than one of the evangelists vouches for its truth. The maniac was at once restored to reason, and was soon found, clothed, and in grateful acknowledgment of the merciful interference of the Lord in his favour, sitting at the feet of Jesus.

A WOMAN CURED OF A BLOODY ISSUE

# A WOMAN CURED OF A BLOODY ISSUE.

"And a woman having an issue of blood twelve years, which had spent all her living upon physicians neither could be healed of any."—LUKE, chap. viii., verses 43.

AFTER THE BIRTH OF CHRIST, 30 YEARS.

THE woman cured of a fatal disease, by touching the garment of the Saviour, furnishes so striking a subject, that many able artists of different countries, and who have lived in different ages, have exerted their powers to bring before us the sufferer, at that glad moment when, her suit preferred, and her unseemly intrusion confessed, she heard the words of mercy.

It is described by Matthew and Mark, as well as St. Luke. All shew that the woman, after long suffering, approached the Lord with great fear; all shew that she aimed at touching his apparel without its being observed, satisfied that, if she could accomplish this, her sufferings would be at an end; and all concur in shewing that the hand of mercy was extended to her, that her pains were no more, and that she was permitted to depart in peace.

## A WOMAN CURED OF A BLOODY ISSUE.

The Evangelists, in dealing with this subject, felt, that while they were taking care that the miracle should be remembered in all time to come, they were also teaching all Christians an important lesson.

From the monitions thus supplied, the trembling sinner learns that it is not the consciousness of his own unworthiness that will forfeit his claim to the compassion of Jesus. Christ will not reject a castaway. Let the sufferer but seek him, as this poor woman did; let the sinner humble himself, but yet feel confident that comfort awaits him, if he can but approach the Redeemer—if he can with sincerity pray that he may be brought in some degree to resemble him—if he can say,

> "Make us of one heart and mind,
> Courteous, pitiful, and kind;
> Lowly, meek, in thought and word,
> Altogether like our Lord;"

then the penitent need not fear but forgiveness will be granted. Faith, combined with humility and a frank confession of our past errors, will not be despised; but with such feelings, if we seek Jesus, he will benignly smile on the lowly suppliant, bid him live here in hope, and finally depart in peace.

CHRIST SENDS FORTH HIS DISCIPLES

# CHRIST SENDS FORTH HIS DISCIPLES.

"And he sent them to preach the kingdom of God and to heal the sick."—LUKE, chap. ix., verse 2.

AFTER THE BIRTH OF CHRIST, 32 YEARS.

THE coming of Christ was to benefit the world, not merely for a short period, during the years which his mortal existence might endure, but for all future times. To this end it was necessary with a view to those days when he would be no more on earth, that faithful ministers should be appointed who would make it their care to spread far and wide a knowledge of his name, and more than that to convey to the world at large those precepts on which their everlasting welfare must depend.

As that awful hour approached in which he was to submit to all the horrors of the cross, he judged it right to regulate the future labours of his disciples.

Having assembled them, he bestowed upon them a portion of that divine power to do good which he derived from his Almighty Father. He charged them to preach the kingdom of

God, and to heal the sick. Their mission was in all respects one of mercy.

He enjoined them not to be over anxious about worldly comforts. They were to take nothing with them on their journey, "neither staves nor scrip, neither bread, neither money; neither have two coats apiece."

Ministers of religion are thus admonished not to indulge a taste for luxury. Those who teach their fellow men "to fix their attention on things above," are not themselves to be the slaves of worldly pleasure.

But while the Lord cautions them against such unworthy yearnings, a solemn notice is given that the faithful servant of the Most High is not to go unrequited of men. Christ told his disciples that in the case of strangers who would not receive them, on going out of the city they were "to shake the very dust from their feet" to be a testimony against men who proved so inhospitable.

While we expect those who preach the word of God to be above sordid cares, we are not meanly to forget that "the labourer is worthy of his hire."

THE GOOD SAMARITAN

# THE GOOD SAMARITAN.

"A certain Samaritan bound up his wounds, pouring in oil and wine, and set him on his own beast."—LUKE, chap. x., verses 33, 34.

AFTER THE BIRTH OF CHRIST, 30 YEARS.

THE priests who were contemporary with Jesus Christ were hungry and exacting. We find in the story of the Good Samaritan a powerful satire on their want of feeling.

The disciples wished to know who they were to regard as neighbours. Christ then told them the following pleasing parable:

A man travelling from Jerusalem to Jericho fell among thieves, who stripped him, wounded him, and left him in the road half dead. There came that way a certain priest who looked on the poor man, but passed on the other side to avoid him. A Levite followed, and did the same. Both left the helpless traveller to fare as he might.

But a Samaritan coming up, took compassion on the sufferer. He bound up his wounds, pouring in oil and wine, set him on his own beast, and brought him to an inn.

Nor was this all. The Good Samaritan gave

# THE GOOD SAMARITAN.

money to the innkeeper to provide what was necessary for the comfort of the traveller, and promised if more should be wanted, to pay any expense that might be incurred on his account when he came that way again.

"Which," Jesus demanded of his disciples, "was neighbour unto him that fell among the thieves?" The Lord himself supplied the answer, "He that shewed mercy on him." Christ impressively added, "Go and do thou likewise."

The beautiful example of charity furnished by the Good Samaritan, ought not to be lost sight of by those who reverence and desire to honour the Redeemer's name. It is not hollow professions of religion that will find favour in the sight of God. The kindly heart that feels for another's woe, is that which his all-seeing eye approves. He who hopes for happiness and heaven, must not suppose respect for words and forms of holiness, will justify him in imitating the priest and the Levite. The sincere Christian will bear in mind the nobler conduct of the Good Samaritan, and feel that to him as well as to the immediate followers of the Lord, those words of benevolence are addressed— "Go thou and do likewise."

THE PRODIGAL SON LEAVES HIS FATHER.

# THE PRODIGAL SON LEAVES HIS FATHER.

"The younger son gathered all together, and took his journey into a far country."—LUKE, chap. xv., verse 13.

WHILE the Saviour wore a mortal form, of all the important lessons which he applied himself to teach mankind, there was none which he was more careful to impress on his followers than that erring man might hope for mercy. He was anxious that the sinner should not become reckless from despair; in other words, he desired "that he should repent and live."

To enforce this, he told, as was his custom, to his disciples a parable.

A certain man, he said, had two sons. Of these, the younger was impatient, as many sons are, that his father should give him at once that portion of his goods which fell to him, or which he understood was to be reserved for him at a future day. The parent, more kind than wise, complied with the demand, made a division of his property, and allowed the youngest son to take his share.

Thus enriched, the youth thought a long career of pleasure lay before him. He took everything that he could claim, and journeyed into a distant country. There, having no prudent father near to caution him against bad companions, he "wasted his substance with riotous living." Acting thus thoughtlessly, he soon became very poor; and, just at the time when his means had begun to fall off, a famine arose in the land. The natural consequence of such a visitation is to make provisions dear; so that the prodigal, after spending his money wastefully, soon found he had not enough left to buy needful food.

He became so distressed, that he hardly knew how to get bread to keep him alive; and he was obliged to seek for some employment, in the hope that the pay he might receive would save him from want. Having no other resource, he applied to a citizen of that country, who consented to find him something to do, and "sent him into his fields to feed swine."

The foolish young man, through wishing too soon to leave the house of his father, and be his own master, was in a short time so miserably reduced, that he was glad to become the hind, or herdsman, of a stranger, and, indeed, a servant or purveyor to beasts of the field.

THE PRODIGAL SON STARVING.

# THE PRODIGAL SON STARVING.

"He would fain have filled his belly with the husks that the swine did eat: and no man gave unto him."—LUKE, chap. xv., verse 16.

---

GREAT was the suffering of the young prodigal. Instead of being in a comfortable home, with a kind father, he found himself in a strange place, among foreigners, with a master over him who cared little for his feelings or his wants. He was indeed placed in so dreadful a situation, that he was almost perishing from hunger. So much did he suffer, that he would gladly have eaten the husks which were provided for the animals it was now his duty to tend; but even this poor fare was not at his command. "No man gave unto him." Due provision was made that the swine should be properly fed; but he who had the charge of them was not allowed to share their food.

How painful must his thoughts have been at that time! Fondly recalling the enjoyment he had known under the parental roof, he contrasted that with the misery which he had brought upon himself. He saw his error; but it was too late.

Thoughtless, headstrong youths, can only

## THE PRODIGAL SON STARVING.

be brought to their senses by pain. The prodigal son was severely punished, but this brought proper reflection; "and when he came to himself, he said, How many hired servants of my father's have bread enough, and to spare, and I perish with hunger. I will arise, and go to my father, and will say unto him, 'Father, I have sinned against heaven and before thee, and am no more worthy to be called thy son; make me as one of thy hired servants.'"

Far from his home, the poor young man felt that even to be a servant in his father's house, would be happiness compared with what he had to endure in the lowly state to which he was reduced, by his culpable wastefulness and folly.

He could now see, that acting ungratefully to a good parent, he had "sinned against heaven." The wealth given to him was gone; that which might have been rendered, by prudence, a benefit, riotous living had made an evil. His pride was sharply, but justly chastised; and hard as he would have deemed such humiliation once, hope could now suggest nothing more desirable, as likely to be within his reach, than that he might be engaged in some menial capacity in his father's house.

THE PRODIGAL SON RETURNS TO HIS FATHER.

# THE PRODIGAL SON RETURNS TO HIS FATHER.

"And he arose and came to his father: but when he was yet a great way off, his father saw him and had compassion, and ran and fell on his neck and kissed him."—LUKE, chap. xv., verse 20.

WHEN sorrow has subdued pride, and made man sensible of his own unworthiness, it is then that he is able to form good resolutions, and to act up to them.

So it was with the prodigal son. With becoming humility he lamented his past errors, and made haste to leave the "far country," to which, in happier days, he had journeyed, to indulge in mirth and revelry. Poor and friendless as he now was, this must have been a sharp trial; and sad misgivings, no doubt, came over him in his dreary and lonely road. He might naturally fear that the parent he had deserted would refuse to receive him again upon any terms. He might expect that he would say—"Ingrate; you have had your fortune; you have left me, to spend it in waste and shameful extravagance; now go to those whose society you preferred to mine: I will have nothing to say to you."

But God has established, for wise purposes,

## THE PRODIGAL SON RETURNS TO HIS FATHER.

compassion for his offspring in the heart of a father. This the prodigal had now the happiness to prove. He had not yet reached the home in which he hoped to be admitted only as a servant, when he was seen afar off by the kind parent, from whom he had been long away. The good man had mourned his son as lost; and, all his misconduct forgotten and forgiven, he ran to meet the prodigal, fell on his neck, and kissed him.

The son then spake, as he had proposed to do, with becoming humility, and said—"Father, I have sinned against heaven and in thy sight, and am no more worthy to be called thy son."

Thus humbled, the good father spared him all harsh reproaches. He ordered his servants to bring forth the best robe, and put it on the penitent; to put a ring on his finger, and shoes on his feet; and to bring the fatted calf, and kill it, that in honour of the son's return, they might eat, drink, and be merry: "for this," said he, "my son, was dead, and is alive again; was lost, and now is found."

From this, Jesus taught, that where there is true repentance, God, our common father, will not reject the wanderer, but will rejoice that he " who was lost, is found."

THE PRODIGALS BROTHER.

# THE PRODIGAL'S BROTHER.

"He called one of the servants, and asked what these things meant."—LUKE, chap. xv., verse 26.

---

THE prodigal had an elder brother: he was a steady young man; he had not called for a share of his father's property, but had remained at home, as a good son should do, happy to assist in the various duties of the farm, which belonged to the old gentleman. When the runaway youth had returned, the other young man, as he came from the field, heard the sound of unwonted mirth; wondered what it could mean, and when he found these rejoicings were on account of the prodigal, who had been so much to blame (having been told what it was all about by a servant), he felt hurt that so much honour should be shown to one who had failed in his duty. "Father," said he, "I have for many years served thee; I have never transgressed thy commandments; yet no fatted calf has been killed for me, and thou never gavest me a kid, that I might make merry with my friends."

The good parent hastened to put aside such repining. "Son," said he, "thou art ever with me, and all that I have is thine. Never-

## THE PRODIGAL'S BROTHER.

theless," he added, "it was meet that we should make merry and be glad; for this thy brother was dead [dead, being lost to his family, he meant], and is alive again [being restored], and was lost, and is found."

And thus Christ taught his disciples shall the mighty Father of all that live cause rejoicing to be made for those who have wandered from the right path, if happily they return to it!

> "While the lamp holds on to burn,
> The vilest sinner may return."

The gracious Saviour of mankind told his followers—"I say unto you, that likewise joy shall be in heaven over one sinner that repenteth, more than over ninety-and-nine just persons, who need no repentance."

Joy is caused by those who seemed to be lost being found again. That joy will be shared by the just and the good. They wish not to be happy alone; and the mercy of the Most High is to them—their minds being enlarged by virtue—a ceaseless source of thankfulness and praise.

THE PHARISEE AND THE PUBLICAN

# THE PHARISEE AND THE PUBLICAN.

"The Pharisee stood and prayed thus with himself, God, I thank thee, that I am not as other men are, extortioners, unjust, adulterers, or even as this publican."—LUKE, chap. xviii., verse 11.

---

THERE are men who think, from attending to certain religious observances, that they are entitled to great favour with the Deity, and look down with contempt on those who, from ignorance or misfortune, are less correct. Christ taught that such arrogance was sinful.

Two men, in illustration of this, he describes to have gone at the same time to the temple. Their object was the same—prayer. One of them was a Pharisee, the other a publican.

The former exulting in the idea he entertained of his own perfection, proudly thanked the God he invoked, for that he was free from the weaknesses and vices of other men, and disdainfully viewing his neighbour, added, " or even as this publican." He further enlarged on his own exemplary conduct, saying, "I fast twice in the week, I give tithes of all I possess."

The unpretending publican could make no such boast. He dared not to approach the

## THE PHARISEE AND THE PUBLICAN.

self-extolling pharisee. Meekly standing "afar off, he would not lift up so much as his eyes to heaven, but smote upon his breast, saying, God be merciful to me a sinner."

The humble heart, which presumes not on its own virtue, but rests its every hope on the benevolence and mercy of the Lord of all, is that which finds favour in the sight of God. "I tell you," said Jesus, speaking unto certain who trusted in themselves that they were righteous, and despised others, that "this man (the publican) went down to his house justified rather than the other:" for, added the Lord, "every one that exalteth himself shall be abased; and he that humbleth himself shall be exalted."

The truly devout will dismiss pride, and study humility. All that florid speech and ostentatious sanctity can offer, will furnish no acceptable tribute to the Supreme Being. From his throne of glory he sees the heart. Our noblest, best aspirations, each ought to feel must be poor in the sight of the Most High, and the best of the sons of men has abundant reason to smite his breast and pray with the publican, "God be merciful to me a sinner!"

CHRIST DISCOURSES WITH HIS DISCIPLES

# CHRIST DISCOURSES WITH HIS DISCIPLES.

"Then he took unto him the twelve, and said unto them, Behold, we go up to Jerusalem, and all things that are written by the prophets concerning the Son of man shall be accomplished."—LUKE, chap. xviii., verse 31.

AFTER THE BIRTH OF CHRIST, 30 YEARS.

It is possible that some of the early followers of Jesus, had taken up the idea, that eventually he would attain worldly greatness, and stand before men as the King of the Jews. He therefore admonished them that if such their thoughts, such their hopes, disappointment awaited them. He wished them not to be self-deceived, and calling them together, he distinctly told them that all things that were written concerning him by the prophets, would be accomplished.

He declared to them, not that he should sit on a throne and distribute honours and costly gifts, but that he should "be delivered unto the Gentiles, be mocked, and spitefully entreated, and spitted on."

Nor was this all, the divine prophet further told, that his cruel enemies should "scourge him and put him to death."

## CHRIST DISCOURSES WITH HIS DISCIPLES.

To this, however, Jesus made the all-important addition "and on the third day he (the Son of man) shall rise again."

Yet to his disciples this was incomprehensible, "They understood none of these things; and the saying was hid from them, neither knew they the things which were spoken."

That which perplexed them is clear to us. We have before us the record of the Saviour's sufferings, which shows that what he predicted was fulfilled to the letter. Cruel men scourged him, mocked his sufferings, and finally suspended him on a cross, to die a death of lingering agony.

On this his melancholy fate as a mortal, we dwell with painful interest. We wonder that men could be so base thus to deal with the mild and beneficent reformer, Jesus. There remains however, behind, the consoling fact, that he rose on the third day from the grave to which he had been consigned, to "sit on the right hand of God." This knowledge is our joy, and enables the grateful Christian with pious exultation to

>"——— talk of all he did and said
>And suffered for us here below;
>The path he marked for us to tread
>And what he's doing for us now."

THE CALLING OF ZACCHEUS

## THE CALLING OF ZACCHÆUS.

"When Jesus came to the place, he looked up, and saw him, and said unto him, Zacchæus, make haste, and come down; for to-day I must abide at thy house."—LUKE, chap. xix., verse 5.

AFTER THE BIRTH OF CHRIST, 30 YEARS.

When Jesus visited Jericho, there lived in that city a man named Zacchæus, who was a rich man, and a chief among the Publicans. He had heard of the Saviour's fame, "and he sought to see Jesus who he was," but being short of stature, his wish could not at first be gratified, in consequence of the throng which pressed around the Lord.

Anxious not to be disappointed, he ran before and climbed up a sycamore tree, "to see Jesus, for he was to pass that way."

When the Lord approached the spot where the tree stood, he looked up and said, "Zacchæus come down, for to-day I must abide in thy house." Zacchæus, upon this, sensible of the honour, hastened to descend, and received the unexpected, unbidden guest joyfully at his home.

There are always some evil-disposed persons ready to find fault without cause, and in this

## THE CALLING OF ZACCHÆUS.

case, an injurious report was raised, that Christ had thought fit to be the guest of one who was a sinner.

Standing before Jesus, Zacchæus said, "Behold, Lord, I give half of my goods to the poor, and if I have taken anything from any man by false accusation, I restore him fourfold."

The Publicans, it has already been explained, were a class of men who farmed the taxes, and Zacchæus, like others in the same situation, was doubtless obliged, in some cases, to act with severity. Jesus was satisfied with what he had stated, and exclaimed, "This day is salvation come to this house, forasmuch as he also is a son of Abraham."

Christ would not condemn Zacchæus because he was spoken ill of by men. He shewed, in going to the Publican's house, that he would not avoid those who anxiously seek him. Let youth who sincerely wish to know the Saviour, seek him with the same earnestness which was shewn by Zacchæus, and they will not seek him in vain. As the Publican climbed the sycamore tree, let them lift themselves above the crowd which oppose their pious desire, so shall salvation come to them.

JUDAS BETRAYS CHRIST

# JUDAS BETRAYS CHRIST.

"And he went his way, and communed with the chief priests and captains, how he might betray him unto them."—LUKE, chap. xxii., verse 4.

AFTER THE BIRTH OF CHRIST, 33 YEARS.

JUDAS, who betrayed the Saviour into the hands of wicked men seeking to put him to a cruel death, was no common wretch. He was a professor of religion, a preacher too, and one of the twelve who had been preferred by Christ to the rest of the world to be his chosen friends. Yet Satan entered into him, corrupted his heart, and disposed him for the love of money to betray his master and his God. Thus, says Dr. Burkitt, we often find in this sinful world "the vilest of sins, the most horrid impieties are committed by men who make the most eminent profession of religion." This base and unworthy conduct is prompted by a love of those worldly pleasures which gold can most readily purchase. Hence it is seen, as we are elsewhere told, that "the love of money is the root of all evil," and therefore Christ enjoined his followers to "take heed and beware of covetousness."

The chief priests and others with whom

## JUDAS BETRAYS CHRIST.

Jesus communed, finding this wicked disposition in one of the apostles, " were glad, and covenanted to give him money. And he promised and sought opportunity to betray him."

The sequel of his melancholy story and his dismal fate, ought to be constantly borne in mind by the serious student. It is desirable that we should be reminded how the traitor was disappointed. The reward he had obtained, he could not enjoy; he carried it back from those to whom he received it, and finally he became a self-murderer.

It cannot be too strongly impressed upon a youthful mind that a desire of gain ought in the outset of life to be confined within moderate limits. Satan now as then finds ready entrance into the avaricious heart. He paints in glowing colours the advantage and delights which money can buy, but these gained by unholy means, fail not to resolve themselves into shame and sorrow, and sometimes, as in the case of the abominable Judas, betray their mad votaries to awful guilt, to vain regrets, and final despair.

CHRIST LED BEFORE THE COUNCIL.

# CHRIST LED BEFORE THE COUNCIL.

"And as soon as it was day, the elders of the people and the chief priests and the scribes came together, and led him into their council."—LUKE, chap. xxii., verse 66.

AFTER THE BIRTH OF CHRIST, 33 YEARS.

BENDING beneath the weight of mortal infirmity, to which he had been content to subject himself in the performance of a great work of mercy, Jesus, pursued by cruel enemies, prayed to his Almighty Father, that if consistent with the decrees of eternal wisdom, the bitter cup of which he was expected to drink, might be removed from him. An angel had appeared to strengthen him, but withal it was not intimated that the sacrifice required could be left incomplete. The Saviour had been forsaken by all, he had been blindfolded, mocked, and blasphemed, when at length, to bring about the last outrage which was to be offered in the name of human justice, Jesus, the day having just dawned after that night of sorrow, was led by the elders, chief priests, and scribes into their council. Then, he was submitted to what in modern phraseology is called an examination. It ran as follows:—

## CHRIST LED BEFORE THE COUNCIL.

*Chief Priests and Elders.* Art thou the Christ? tell us.

*Jesus.* If I tell you ye will not believe; and if I also ask you, ye will not answer me, nor let me go. Hereafter shall the Son of Man sit on the right hand of the power of God.

*Chief Priests and others.* Art thou then the Son of God?

*Jesus.* I am.

Those in whose presence he stood, affected to think this sufficient to justify them in condemning him to death, and the cry they raised was to the effect—"we need no further enquiry, no further witnesses, for he himself has done that which is equal to a confession of guilt. From himself we have heard that he is the Son of God."

The multitude then arose, and "led him unto Pilate." There they accused Jesus of "perverting the nation." Pilate interrogated the prisoner himself, and the result was "he could find no fault in that man."

But the feelings excited against Christ could not be appeased. His enemies were the more fierce against him. They pursued him with senseless rancour, and caused him to suffer extreme agony; agony which was to constitute his glory and accomplish man's salvation.

CHRIST CRUCIFIED.

# CHRIST CRUCIFIED.

"And when they were come to the place, which is called Calvary, there they crucified him, and the malefactors, one on the right hand, and the other on the left."—LUKE, chap. xxiii., verse 33.

AFTER THE BIRTH OF CHRIST, 33 YEARS.

THE circumstantial account written by St. Luke of the death of the Redeemer, presents many incidents of a most affecting character. Though Pontius Pilate could find no fault in Jesus, when the fierce cry of "crucify him," was raised, he suffered himself to be overpowered by clamour, and "gave sentence as was required."

Christ offered no resistance. Prepared to go "like a lamb to the slaughter," his meek submission interested some females who were among the crowd, and who saw him on his way to the place of execution, so much that "they bewailed and lamented him." He marked their sorrow, and turning to them spoke as follows:—"Daughters of Jerusalem, weep not for me, but weep for yourselves and for your children." He added, mournful days were approaching when those who lived should be disposed "to say to the mountains fall on us, and to the hills cover us."

## CHRIST CRUCIFIED.

Arrived at Calvary, the Son of God was crucified between two convicted malefactors. His patience and love for mankind, even in that dismal hour, were strongly marked in the affecting prayer which he breathed for his tormentors: "Father, forgive them, they know not what they do."

The people gazed on him with surprise, and the rulers and soldiers mocked, by calling to him to save himself if he were "the chosen of God," "the King of the Jews,"

One of his companions in suffering spoke to him reproachfully, requiring him if he were Christ, to save himself and them. The other malefactor reproved the first, and remarked that they (the two thieves) suffered but the due reward of their deeds, while Jesus had done nothing amiss. Then addressing the Saviour he prayed, "Lord remember me when thou comest unto thy kingdom." To him Christ gave the gracious and consoling answer, "To-day shalt thou be with me in paradise."

Unwonted gloom came over the earth, the sun was darkened, and the veil of the temple rent. "Father, into thy hands I commend my spirit, Jesus cried with a loud voice, and gave up the ghost."

THE ENTOMBMENT OF JESUS.

# THE ENTOMBMENT OF JESUS.

"This man went unto Pilate, and begged the body of Jesus. And he took it down, and wrapped it in linen, and laid it in a sepulchre that was hewn in stone, wherein never man before was laid."—LUKE, chap. xxiii., verses 52, 53.

AFTER THE BIRTH OF CHRIST, 33 YEARS.

WHEN the mortal anguish of Christ had ceased, and Jesus slept in death, a man named Joseph, a counsellor, of whom it is said "he was a good man and a just," begged his body from Pilate. He was of Arimathæa, and though a member of the council, had not given his sanction to the monstrous treatment of Jesus. As Joseph had not been able to save the blameless sufferer from the punishment of the cross, he was anxious now to do all that charity could offer, to give the mangled remains honourable burial.

Having this object in view, Joseph waited on Pilate, and his suit being granted, he proceeded to mount Calvary, to the cross on which the bleeding form of the Lord was still suspended. Joseph "took it down, and laid it in a sepulchre."

This took place on the Friday. The Jewish sabbath which commences after sun-set on

## THE ENTOMBMENT OF JESUS.

that day, drew near, when women who had come with Christ from Galilee appeared. The circumstances of our Lord's interment, says Burkitt, as recorded by the Evangelist present " such a funeral as never was since graves were first digged. Where, observe, first our Lord's body must be begged before it could be buried; the dead bodies of malefactors being in the power, and at the disposal of the judge that condemned them. Observe, secondly, the person that begged his body and bestowed a decent and honourable funeral upon it; Joseph of Arimathæa, a worthy though a close disciple. Grace doth not always make a public and open show where it is: but as there is much secret treasure in the bowels of the earth unseen, so there is much grace in the hearts of some saints, which the world takes little notice of."

This is a just and a true remark of the pious divine. Christ himself tells us " it is not every one that cries Lord, Lord, that shall enter his kingdom."

WOMEN VIEWING THE SEPULCHRE

# WOMEN VIEWING THE SEPULCHRE.

"And the women also, which came with him from Galilee, followed after, and beheld the sepulchre, and how his body was laid."—LUKE, chap. xxiii., verse 55.

AFTER THE BIRTH OF CHRIST, 33 YEARS.

ATTENTION has already been drawn to the striking fact, that while the hearts of men were closed against the great prophet, who came to save them, women pitied his sorrows and were anxious to relieve his sufferings. "O woman," he in his dreary pilgrimage might have exclaimed in the words of an admired poet of our own times—

"When stern affliction clouds the brow
A ministering angel thou."

With tearful eye women gazed on the last agonies of the illustrious victim, and with gentle reverence they followed his remains to the grave. Then having seen "how that his body was laid," they procured spices and ointments to be deposited by his side.

"The grave or sepulchre," remarks a learned commentator already quoted, "in which our Lord lay, was hewn out of rock; that so his enemies might have no occasion to say that his disciples stole him away by secret holes and unseen passages under ground: it was in a new sepulchre wherein never man was laid before, lest his adversaries should say that it was another that was risen, who was buried there before him." He further remarks, "The manner of our Lord's funeral was hasty, open, and decent. Hasty, because of the preparations for the sabbath; open, that all persons might be spectators, and none might say he was buried before he was dead; decent, being wrapped up in fine linen, and perfumed with spices."

But it has been held by eminent divines, that the Son of God, being thus consigned to a dreary tomb, was to prove that Christ could conquer death even in his own territories and dominions, while the apparent depth of his humiliation showed to what his love for sinners could bring him, for their benefit and salvation. "The grave," writes Burkitt, "could not long keep Christ, it shall not always keep Christians. Awake, and sing thou that dwellest in the dust, for the enmity of the grave is slain in Christ."

CHRIST AT EMMAUS

# CHRIST AT EMMAUS.

"And their eyes were opened, and they knew him; and he vanished out of their sight."—LUKE, chap. xxiv., verse 31.

AFTER THE BIRTH OF CHRIST, 33 YEARS.

AFTER Jesus had been crucified, two of the disciples journeying to Emmaus, a village not far from Jerusalem, as they walked along discoursing with each other on recent events—on the death and resurrection of their Lord—it came to pass that a stranger drew near, and joined conversation with them. "What manner of communications, said he, are these that ye have one to another, as ye walk, and are sad?" One of them, whose name was Cleopas, "answering, said unto him, Art thou only a stranger in Jerusalem, and hast not known the things which are come to pass there in these days? And he said unto them, what things? and they said, concerning Jesus of Nazareth, which was a prophet mighty in deed and word before God and all the people."

Then they spake of the condemnation, the crucifixion, and the resurrection of the Redeemer. Withal they expressed misgivings, saying, "we trusted that it had been he which should have redeemed Israel."

## CHRIST AT EMMAUS.

The stranger upon this reproved them, and said, "O fools, and slow of heart to believe all that the prophets have spoken: Ought not Christ to have suffered these things, and to enter into his glory?" Beginning at Moses and the prophets, he went on "to expound in all the Scriptures" the things concerning Jesus.

Thus engaged, they drew near to the village, when the stranger "made as though he would have gone further," but they pressed him to stay with them, as the day was far spent.

He turned at their request, and, as he sat with them, he took bread and blessed it, and gave to them. Then their eyes were opened; they knew the stranger who had been with them was Christ. They recalled with interest and delight his discourse, and said, "Did not our heart burn within us while he talked with us by the way;" they felt that they had been blessed indeed, to listen to their Lord "while he opened to them the Scriptures."

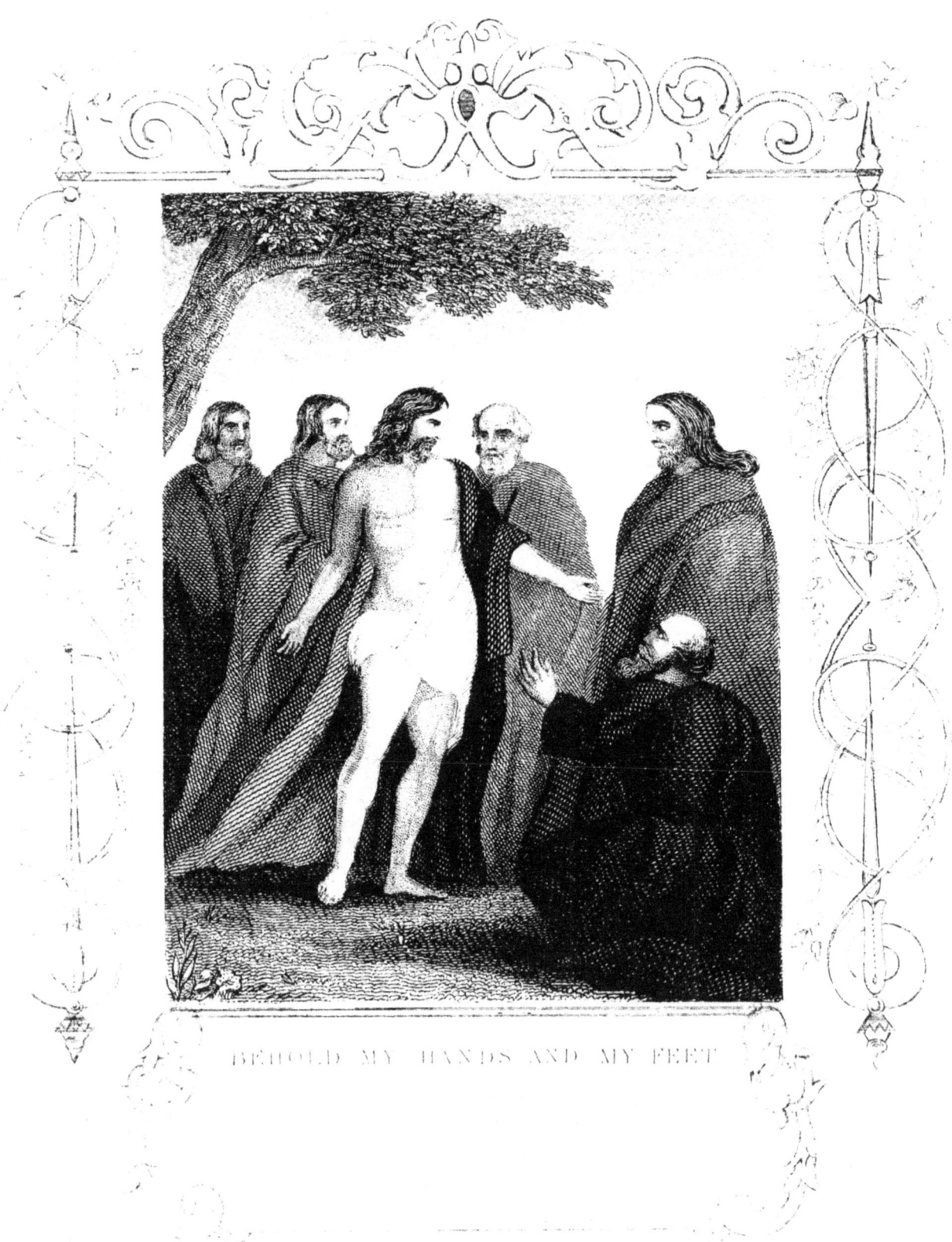

BEHOLD MY HANDS AND MY FEET

# BEHOLD MY HANDS, AND MY FEET.

"Behold my hands and my feet, that it is I myself: handle me, and see; for a spirit hath not flesh and bones, as ye see me have."—LUKE, chap. xxiv., verse 39.

AFTER THE BIRTH OF CHRIST, 33 YEARS.

IT will easily be conceived that the amazement of the two disciples at Emmaus, was great in the extreme. The more they reflected on what had occurred, the more they were astonished. To have seen one who had risen from the dead, that one their crucified master, and to have been enlightened by the wisdom of a teacher they had seen laid in the grave, was so wonderfully important, that late as the hour was, they determined on returning forthwith immediately to Jerusalem. Thither they proceeded, where they found the eleven chosen followers of Christ, their minds occupied by the extraordinary things they had heard, assembled together. They told each other of what had been seen, when, while they were speaking, Jesus stood in the midst of them, and said, "Why are ye troubled? and why do thoughts arise in your hearts? Behold my hands and my feet, that it is I myself." They could

## BEHOLD MY HANDS, AND MY FEET.

scarcely believe the evidence of their senses, but Christ, desirous that no doubt should remain on their minds, added, "handle me and see; for a spirit hath not flesh and bones, as you see me have."

From this it will be seen that it was really the wounded mortal body of Jesus, which was reanimated. Of that he gave the disciples a further proof, by eating of a broiled fish and a honeycomb in their presence.

Having done so much to remove all doubt as to the reality of his being recalled to life, he reminded them of what he had formerly taught, that all things must be fulfilled which were written in the law of Moses, and in the prophets, and in the Psalms, concerning him. This he earnestly pressed upon them, and then having given them his blessing, "he was parted from them, and carried up into heaven."

A spectacle so touching and sublime requires no comment. The mind can but imperfectly contemplate it. How must those who beheld it have been moved with wonder, joy, and gratitude!

THE LAMB OF GOD

# THE LAMB OF GOD.

"The next day John seeth Jesus coming unto him, and saith, Behold the Lamb of God, which taketh away the sin of the world."—JOHN, chap. i., verse 29.

AFTER THE BIRTH OF CHRIST, 30 YEARS.

FROM a very remote period, indeed from the creation, it had been customary to offer sacrifices to God. When the children of Jacob had become a great nation, priests and prophets regulated the various sacrifices, which it was deemed fitting to offer on particular occasions, to invoke a blessing, or to atone for transgression. When some great sin had been committed against the majesty of the Eternal, a victim of singular purity, was required by the Jewish law.

John the Baptist, was a highly gifted man. His piety, and the life he led in the wilderness, had gained him great consideration, but he announced to his countrymen that he "was but the voice of one crying in the wilderness, Make straight the way of the Lord." When those sent to question him by the Pharisees were about him, he told them that "one stood among them far greater than he; one whose shoe's latchet he was not worthy to unloose."

## THE LAMB OF GOD.

It was at Bethabara that John made this remarkable revelation, and on the following day, seeing Jesus coming to him, he exclaimed, "Behold the Lamb of God, which taketh away the sin of the world."

Thus we see it was given to this eminent man to foretel the approach of Christ, and to point to him, though previously unknown, as the lamb for sacrifice, whose surpassing purity would expiate the mournful wanderings of a guilty world. He further proclaimed that he had "seen the spirit descending from heaven like a dove," and he who had sent him (John) to baptize with water, had said, "Upon whom thou shalt see the Spirit descending, and remaining on him, the same is he which baptizeth with the Holy Ghost." The Spirit he had seen abide on Jesus, and therefore, "he bare record that he was the Son of God."

The testimony of John is the more unexceptionable as it goes to humble himself. Wise and pious as he was, his ambition soared no higher than to announce the coming of one far greater than he could pretend to be.

THE MARRIAGE AT CANA

# THE MARRIAGE AT CANA.

"And the third day there was a marriage in Cana of Galilee; and the mother of Jesus was there."—JOHN, chap. ii., verse 1.

AFTER THE BIRTH OF CHRIST 30 YEARS.

THOUGH from the course of events, and in fulfilment of what had been foretold by the prophets of Israel, Christ was a "man of sorrow," he did not refuse, when invited, to attend a public entertainment. "He went," says Burkitt, "not so much for the pleasure of eating, as for the purpose of conversing and doing good." When the marriage at Cana was to take place, he condescended to grace it with his presence. Some have supposed that in this instance, St. John was the bridegroom, others that one of the parties was related to the Virgin Mary, as she is stated to have been of the company; but whoever the newly-married couple might be, Christ in appearing at the feast, and performing there his first miracle, meant to do honour to the ordinance of marriage. It is an ancient and solemn ceremony, and marriage, says the apostle, "is honourable among all."—Heb. xiii. 4.

Feasting on such an occasion in moderation,

## THE MARRIAGE AT CANA.

the Lord saw was proper, and when the wine provided for the refreshment of the guests at Cana was exhausted, he ordered six water-pots, which, according to the Jewish usage, were there set apart, to be filled with water. These pots contained each two or three firkins, and being filled, he directed that they should be borne to the governor of the feast, and he, having tasted what was thus set before him, found the water had been changed into wine. The governor then called the bridegroom, and said, "Every man at the beginning doth set forth good wine, and when men have well drunk, that which is worse: but thou hast kept the good wine even until now."

From this we see that moderately to enjoy the good things of this life, on proper occasions, and with a grateful heart, is not sinful. He who gave us being, never designed that life should be a cheerless scene of sorrow. From the example of Christ we are taught what Dr. Watts has expounded, that

"Religion never was designed
To make our pleasures less."

CHRIST AND THE WOMAN OF SAMARIA.

# CHRIST AND THE WOMAN OF SAMARIA.

"There cometh a woman of Samaria to draw water; Jesus saith unto her, give me to drink."—JOHN, chap. iv., verse 7.

AFTER THE BIRTH OF CHRIST, 30 YEARS.

THE detailed account which John gives of Christ's interview with the woman of Samaria, deserves to be read with especial attention, from the evidence it offers of his humble, if not distressed condition; of his goodness, power, and more than human knowledge. Asking so small a boon as a drop of water to quench his thirst, the woman was astonished that a Jew should presume to expect such a thing from a woman of Samaria. He replied, that had she known his quality, and applied to him, he would have given her living water—such water that those who drank of it should never thirst again.

Upon that the woman desired to have some of the water of which he spoke. He desired her to call her husband, when she replied that she had none. Jesus then proved, though it does not appear he had ever seen her before, that it would have been in vain to attempt

## CHRIST AND THE WOMAN OF SAMARIA.

deception; he told her that she spoke truth; that she had had five husbands, and was then living with a man who was not her husband!

Then the woman exclaimed, " Sir, I perceive that thou art a prophet.' Christ foretold that the hour was at hand when the true worshippers should worship the Father in spirit and in truth. He added, "the Father seeketh such to worship him. God is a spirit, and they that worship him must worship him in spirit and in truth."

We are hence to understand, that we must, desiring to propitiate him, worship him, not with vain forms, but spiritually, with filial reverence and holy awe. This Christ taught the woman of Samaria, and he distinctly declared to her that he was the Messiah. The announcement so astonished the woman, that we read she " left her water-pot, and went her way into the city, and saith to the men, Come see a man who told me all things that ever I did : Is not this the Christ?"

She felt; she confessed the divinity of Jesus. May those who read her story profit from the lesson she received, and "worship God in spirit and in truth."

CHRIST CURING THE NOBLEMAN'S SON

# CHRIST CURING THE NOBLEMAN'S SON.

"Jesus saith unto him, go thy way; thy son liveth. And the man believed the word that Jesus had spoken unto him, and he went his way."—JOHN, chap. iv., verse 50.

AFTER THE BIRTH OF CHRIST, 30 YEARS.

ALL the evangelists tell of the astonishing cures performed by Jesus, but for the most part his miracles were wrought in favour of the helpless and the poor. St. John writes, that one who sought comfort at his hands was of high quality. He reports that at Cana, in Galilee, there was a certain nobleman whose son was sick at Capernaum, and who, hearing that Jesus was journeying that way, "out of Judea into Galilee," he went to him and besought him "that he would come down and heal his son, who was at the point of death." Jesus said to him, "Except ye see signs and wonders, ye will not believe." The nobleman repeated his anxious request, and said, "Sir, come down ere my child die."

What follows is very interesting. Christ said to the nobleman, "Go thy way, thy son liveth." St. John adds, "And the man believed the word that Jesus had spoken unto

## CHRIST CURING THE NOBLEMAN'S SON.

him, and he went his way." And as he was now going down, his servants met him, and told him, saying, thy son liveth. Then enquired he of them the hour when he began to amend; and they said unto him, yesterday, at the seventh hour the fever left him. So the father knew that it was at the same hour in which Jesus said unto him, thy son liveth: and himself believed, and his whole house."

It will be remarked, this nobleman had such an opinion of Christ's power that he journeyed a considerable way to see him, when he heard of his coming to Galilee. So much we collect from the fact, that it was not till the day after Christ had spoken the healing word, that he, by returning to his home and finding his son healed, could test its efficacy. He had appealed to Christ as a father would to a human physician, and entreated him to visit the sufferer, that he might judge of the case and exercise his skill. Christ gave him the soothing assurance that his son lived. Happily he was able to believe it. He had faith, and through faith he rejoiced in finding his fondest hopes realized. The son was spared to the enjoyment of mortal life, and the father believing with all his house in the Saviour saw a blessed eternity open before him.

CHRIST CURING THE IMPOTENT MAN.

# CHRIST CURING THE IMPOTENT MAN.

"And immediately the man was made whole, and took up his bed and walked: and on the same day was the sabbath."—JOHN, chap. v., verse 9.

AFTER THE BIRTH OF CHRIST, 30 YEARS.

JESUS CHRIST, in the performance of duty, did not regard those observances which the pharisees and others deemed of immense importance, more especially when they stood in the way of his doing good, and relieving pain.

There was a certain man who had suffered from infirmity during thirty-eight years. Jesus being made acquainted with his case, addressed the question to him, "Wilt thou be made whole?" The unfortunate then rested near the pool of Bethesda, and told the Lord that he had no one to aid him when the water was troubled, so as to enable him to reach its healing waves; but while he, feeble as he was, attempted to approach it, others got before him, and he still found himself excluded from the benefit. Jesus upon that told him to rise, take up his bed and walk, which, being then made whole, he immediately did.

This took place on the Sabbath-day, and the

## CHRIST CURING THE IMPOTENT MAN.

Jews therefore told the man who had been cured, that it was not lawful for him to carry his bed on the sabbath. His reply was, that he who had made him whole directed him to do so. They multiplied their inquiries as to who it was that had performed this miracle; but "he that was healed wist not who it was," for he knew not the person of Jesus, who had withdrawn to avoid the crowd there assembled. Christ again saw the man in the temple, and cautioned him, since his health was restored, to be careful and "sin no more."

The man afterwards told the Jews, that it was Jesus that had made him whole, and therefore they sought to persecute the Saviour, and to kill him. Their perverted understandings led them to think he was unworthy to live, because he had cured sickness on the sacred day. Jesus answered, "My Father worked hitherto, and I work." They were still more disposed to assail him then, for declaring God to be his Father. Jesus upon this expostulated with them, and distinctly stated the power of the Father to be given to the Son, and as God could raise the dead, the Saviour could quicken whom he pleased to awaken to the light of immortal truth.

CHRIST FEEDING THE MULTITUDE

# CHRIST FEEDING THE MULTITUDE.

"When Jesus then lifted up his eyes, and saw a great company come unto him, he saith unto Philip, whence shall we buy bread, that these may eat."—JOHN, chap. vi., verse 5.

AFTER THE BIRTH OF CHRIST, 30 YEARS.

ONE of the great delights of the Saviour while on earth, was to feed the hungry. Followed by a multitude, he went up into a mountain and sat with his disciples. The Jewish feast of the passover was at hand, and pitying the crowd he saw near him, who wanted food, he said to Philip, "Whence shall we buy bread, that these may eat?" "This he said," the evangelist John tells us, "to prove Philip," as he knew in his own mind what he would do. He was answered by Philip, "Two hundred penny-worth of bread is not sufficient for them, that every one of them may take a little." Andrew, Simon Peter's brother, then said, "There is a lad here that hath five barley loaves and two small fishes, but what are they among so many?"

Jesus directed that the men who had followed him should sit down. There was much grass in that place, and the men in consequence of the directions thus given, seated themselves, being five thousand in number. Christ then took the five barley loaves, and when he had given thanks, he distributed to the disciples, and they gave to them that were set down: and likewise of the fishes as much as they would." When their hunger was appeased, he said to his disciples, "Gather up the fragments that remain, that nothing be lost." These they collected, and "filled twelve baskets with the fragments of the five barley loaves which remained over and above unto them that had eaten."

Conviction was carried to the hearts of the crowd by the relief which had been so bounteously afforded. Christ blessed the loaves before he distributed them, thus teaching men that when about to share the comforts provided for them by their eternal Father, they ought not thoughtlessly and thanklessly to enjoy the benefit, without devoutly raising their thoughts in gratitude to the Giver of all good. While we find our daily sustenance almost as miraculously, quite as graciously supplied as it was to the crowd who followed the Lord, we ought not to take it as a matter of course: our hearts ought to expand with gratitude and love.

THE WOMAN TAKEN IN ADULTERY

# THE WOMAN TAKEN IN ADULTERY.

"And the scribes and Pharisees brought unto him (Jesus) a woman taken in adultery."—JOHN, chap. viii., verse 3.

AFTER THE BIRTH OF CHRIST, 30 YEARS.

CHRIST held in great contempt the proud Pharisees. They presumed to think that none were so virtuous as they were, and they applied themselves with especial industry to punish the vices and the weaknesses of others, while secretly they indulged in great excesses.

On one occasion they brought to him a woman who was accused of very bad conduct, for which they said, under the law of Moses, she would be stoned to death.

Jesus never favoured sin, but he pitied the unhappy. When he saw a poor woman in the hands of cruel men, he regarded her with compassion, and the accusers having told him what the law required, wished to know how he would visit the offender. They flattered themselves that they had him on what is called the horns of a dilemma, from which there was no escape. If he favoured the prisoner, he would offend the law; and if he vindicated

## THE WOMAN TAKEN IN ADULTERY.

the law, he must aid their inhuman design. So they thought, but they deceived themselves. After a pause, as though he heard them not, on the question being repeated, Jesus signified that he was content that the law should take its course, but added, "He that is without sin among you let him first cast a stone at her." This powerful rebuke they could not endure. They saw that they were known; each was conscious that abiding by this command or direction, he could not take part in the execution; so they stole away, going out one by one, the eldest first, and then down to the youngest, for all were sinners.

He had seemed to write on the ground while they withdrew. Raising himself he saw the woman alone, and said to her, "Where are thine accusers? hath no man condemned thee?" She said, "No man, Lord!" Jesus then said to her, "Neither do I condemn thee, go and sin no more."

In this scene the student will note Christ's generous opposition to cold-blooded cruelty; his rebuke, as keen as it was gentle, to make them ashamed of their malice; and finally his tenderness for the accused, in forbearing to condemn for the past, while admonishing her for the future to sin no more.

MARTHA MEETS JESUS

# MARTHA MEETS JESUS.

"Then when Mary was come where Jesus was, and saw him, she fell down at his feet, saying unto him, Lord, if thou hadst been here, my brother had not died."—JOHN, chap. xi., verse 32.

AFTER THE BIRTH OF CHRIST, 30 YEARS.

Jesus loved Martha, and Mary, and their brother Lazarus. When he heard that the last was sick, having remained two days in the place where he then was, he prepared to visit Judea again, remarking, "Our friend Lazarus sleepeth, but I go to awake him out of his sleep."

The disciples expressed a hope, that if Lazarus slept he would do well, but Jesus then told them that he was dead, and of this he said he was glad, for their sake: as it would enable them to believe in that power which was now to be exerted with such miraculous effect.

Coming to Bethany, Jesus found that Lazarus had been four days in the grave. Martha, when she heard Christ was near, advanced to meet him, and "Lord," said she, affectionately lamenting the loss she had sustained, "if thou hadst been here, my brother had not died.

## MARTHA MEETS JESUS.

But I know that even now, whatsoever thou wilt ask of God, God will give thee."

"Thy brother shall rise again," said Jesus. The sister of Lazarus replied, "I know that he shall rise again in the resurrection, at the last day." The speech of Martha called forth the solemn and most important declaration of the Son of God, "I am the resurrection and the life: he that believeth in me, though he were dead, yet shall he live: and whosoever liveth and believeth in me shall never die."

The sisters wept, and some Jews to whom Lazarus had been known, wept also. Jesus groaned in the spirit, was troubled, and several who were present said, "could not this man, which opened the eyes of the blind, have caused that even this man should not have died?"

Christ asked where the body of Lazarus had been laid, and was asked to "Come and see." To the grave he then proceeded. There it was, that he had purposed to give a striking proof of what he had told Martha, "I am the resurrection and the life: he that believeth in me, though he were dead, yet shall he live."

RAISING OF LAZARUS

# RAISING OF LAZARUS.

"And he that was dead came forth, bound hand and foot with graveclothes: and his face was bound about with a napkin. Jesus saith unto them, loose him, and let him go."—JOHN, chap. xi., verse 44.

AFTER THE BIRTH OF CHRIST, 31 YEARS.

CHRIST groaned repeatedly while contemplating the case of Lazarus. It was, probably, in pity for the distress of the sisters of the departed, rather than for Lazarus, whom he had resolved to wake from the sleep of death. Having been led to the grave, he directed that the stone should be taken away. Martha offered some objections, on account of the supposed state of the corpse. For doing so he gently reproved her, in these words: "Said I not unto thee, that if thou wouldest believe, thou shouldest see the glory of God?"

Now the moment had arrived when the great work he contemplated was to be performed. The stone was taken away from the place where the dead man was laid, and Jesus, lifting up his eyes, said, "Father, I thank thee, that thou hast heard me. And I know that thou hearest me always; but because of the people which

## RAISING OF LAZARUS.

stand by I said it, that they may believe that thou hast sent me."

Having thus appealed to the Almighty God of Heaven and earth, Jesus cried with a loud voice, "Lazarus come forth."

These words were no sooner spoken, than, to the amazement of Martha, Mary, and all who heard them, "he that was dead came forth, bound hand and foot, with grave clothes; and his face was bound about with a napkin." Jesus then said to the beholders, "Loose him, and let him go."

It was not the custom of that country to bury those who died in coffins. They were commonly enveloped in a winding-sheet when committed to the earth, and Lazarus appears to have been thus encumbered, when, at the voice of the son of God, he burst from the thraldrom and darkness of the grave, again to appear among the living. "If," writes an eminent divine, "Lazarus did thus instantly start up at the voice of Christ in the day of his humiliation, how shall the dead be roused up out of their graves, by that voice which will shake the frame of heaven, and move the foundations of the earth, in the day of his glorification!"

MARY ANOINTING THE FEET OF JESUS

# MARY ANOINTING THE FEET OF JESUS.

"Then took Mary a pound of ointment of spikenard, very costly, and anointed the feet of Jesus, and wiped his feet with her hair: and the house was filled with the odour of the ointment."—JOHN, chap. xii., verse 3.

AFTER THE BIRTH OF CHRIST, 32 YEARS.

SOMETIME after the miracle which raised Lazarus from the dead, Jesus being at Bethany was at a supper which had been made for him. Lazarus and some of the disciples were with him, and Martha served the guests.

On this occasion, it appears, Mary took a pound of ointment of spikenard, which was very costly, and anointed the feet of Jesus, wiping them with her hair, as the woman had done in the Pharisee's house at Nain.

That the ointment was indeed valuable, seems proved by the fact next stated, that the house was filled with its odour, and thereupon Judas Iscariot thought fit to blame the waste which had been made, as it appeared to him, and he asked, "Why that which had been poured on the feet of the Saviour had not been sold for three hundred pence, and given to the poor?"

## MARY ANOINTING THE FEET OF JESUS.

To be charitable to the poor is certainly a duty, but could too much honour be rendered to such a guest as Jesus? It was not benevolence that moved Judas to complain. He, a base and cruel man, cared not for the poor, but having been permitted to carry the bag, in other words, having been entrusted with the little all of the disciples, he thought the addition of such a sum as three hundred pence would be very agreeable. This it was that prompted him, thief as we are told by St. John he was, to complain of what had been done.

At that moment Jesus knew that his stay in this world would be short. He addressed no cutting reproach to Judas, but he restrained his rude speech, saying, "Let her alone; against the day of my burying hath she kept this. The poor," said he, "always ye have with you, but me ye have not always."

It was thus he intimated that the time had nearly come when, for mortal transgressions, he, the Son of God, was to suffer on the cross.

CHRIST WASHING THE DISCIPLES FEET

# CHRIST WASHING THE DISCIPLES' FEET.

"After that he poureth water into a bason, and began to wash the disciples' feet, and to wipe them with the towel wherewith he was girded."—JOHN, chap. xiii., verse 5.

AFTER THE BIRTH OF CHRIST, 33 YEARS.

CHRIST was a pattern of humility. The foolish arrogance which men often display was never seen in him. With the poorest, with the most degraded he was not ashamed to converse, and the humblest office he was content to perform.

This was seen in what passed a short time before he was betrayed into the hands of those who sought his life.

The feast of the passover was at hand, and we are told "he knew that his hour was come." Those the Father had given to him he loved to the end, and having supped with his disciples, one of whom the evil one had moved to join with the enemy of our Lord, Jesus, knowing "that the Father had given all things into his hands, and that he was come from God, and went to God," was desirous of teaching those about him yet one more important lesson. He poured water into a bason, washed the feet of his disciples, and wiped them "with the towel wherewith he was girded."

St. Peter was reluctant to see Jesus thus humble himself, and said, "Thou shalt never wash my feet." The reply of Christ was, "If I wash thee not, thou hast no part in me." These words at once made Peter sensible of his condition. He felt that it was only by the Saviour that he could be effectually cleansed from sin, and he then said, "Lord, not my feet only, but also my hands and my head."

Afterwards Christ taught those who called him Master, to bear in mind the example which he had set them: "Ye call me Master and Lord," he said; "and ye say well; for so I am. If I then, your Lord and Master, have washed your feet; ye also ought to wash one another's feet." The youthful christian will understand that the sincere followers of Christ are ever ready to administer to each other's comfort. Were this rule universally borne in mind, and acted upon, how largely would the discord and misery now witnessed in the world be abated!

JESUS GOING FORTH WITH HIS DISCIPLES.

# JESUS GOING FORTH WITH HIS DISCIPLES.

"Jesus went forth with his disciples over the brook Cedron, where was a garden, into the which he entered, and his disciples."—JOHN, chap. xviii. verse 1.

AFTER THE BIRTH OF CHRIST, 33 YEARS.

WE learn from the narrative of St. John, that Jesus "oft-times resorted to a garden near the brook of Cedron." The garden was called Gethsemane, a place celebrated through every Christian land, as that in which the Saviour's dying agonies may be said to have commenced; as that in which he was to be betrayed into the hands of those who thirsted for his blood, by the perfidious Judas.

St. Matthew and St. Luke give details of the circumstances under which the faithless one accomplished his object. These have been described in former pages. John's report is valuable, as confirmatory of their statements, but it has, moreover, the merit of bringing before us the divine prayer which Christ breathed immediately before he bent his steps towards the garden. Aware that his mortal existence was about to close, he raised his voice to implore the Eternal Father that those

## JESUS GOING FORTH WITH HIS DISCIPLES.

who had been given to him, might have his joy fulfilled in themselves. He prayed not that they might be taken out of the world, but that they might be kept from evil; that they might be sanctified through the word of truth.

It is not a little important to remark, that while thus preferring a petition to his glorious Father for those who were his immediate followers, he at the same time prayed for us, for us who were to live many ages after his mortal sufferings had closed. Having spoken of those to whom he had given the word, he proceeded, "Neither pray I for these alone, but for them also who shall believe in me through their word: that they all may be one, as thou Father art in me, and I in thee."

For *us*, for *all* who believe in his name, in that night of sorrow, the suffering Jesus fervently prayed. Those who read that prayer with due attention, it is hardly too much to suppose will be eager to fly to the Saviour—

"Swift as the morning light,
Lest life's young golden beams should die
In sudden endless night."

CHRIST LED BEFORE PILATE.

# CHRIST LED FORTH BY PILATE.

"Then came Jesus forth, wearing the crown of thorns, and the purple robe. And Pilate saith unto them, Behold the man!"—JOHN, chap. xix., verse 5.

AFTER THE BIRTH OF CHRIST, 33 YEARS.

THE four Evangelists relate the sufferings of Jesus, and on all the leading points their agreement is perfect; but it is in the Gospel of St. John that we find the most complete report of the incidents which immediately followed his arrest, and the surrender of him to the Jews.

Those who had Jesus in custody, carried him to the judgment-hall. Pontius Pilate there inquired what charge they had to prefer against him. They evaded the question by saying, "If he had not been a malefactor, they would not have brought him there." Not wishing to have anything to do with the case, Pilate told them to judge the prisoner according to the Jewish law. Such a concession was not satisfactory, because under their law he could not be put to death.

Pilate had left the judgment-hall, but he now re-entered it, and said to Jesus, "Art thou the king of the Jews?" Christ replied to this by asking if Pilate had put the question

## CHRIST LED FORTH BY PILATE.

to him of himself, or if others had prompted it? and afterwards explained, saying, "My kingdom is not of this world: if my kingdom were of this world, then would my servants fight, that I should not be delivered to the Jews: but now is my kingdom not from hence."

Christ, as already related, was by Pilate subjected to the scourge. His sufferings moved no pity, but "the soldiers platted a crown of thorns, and put it on his head, and they put on him a purple robe, and said, Hail, king of the Jews! and they smote him with their hands."

Again Pilate spoke in favour of the prisoner. "Behold," said he, "I bring him forth to you, that ye may know that I find no fault in him." Then it was that Jesus came forth, wearing the crown of thorns, and the purple robe, and Pilate said to them, "Behold the man!"

Thus was Christ subjected, even by the governor who proclaimed him faultless, to the heartless mockery of a bloodthirsty crew. All this, and more than all, the Son of God, was content to endure in solemn expiation of the sins of men. The heir of immortal glory submitted, in the cause of men's salvation, to be insulted and punished like the meanest human offender against the laws.

# CHRIST SCOURGED.

"Then Pilate therefore took Jesus and scourged him."—JOHN, chap. xix., verse 1.

AFTER THE BIRTH OF CHRIST, 33 YEARS.

INGENIOUS cruelty laboured to make the last hours of Jesus as painful as possible. It was not enough to deprive him of life, and by the most horrible punishment, as heretofore described, of the cross, but preliminary torments and shocking indignities were heaped on the unoffending victim, that the cup of which he was to drink, might be rendered one of all-surpassing bitterness. Though Pilate could find nothing to condemn in the conduct of Christ; though personally he was not indisposed to save him, officially he thought himself bound to listen to those who sought the Lord's destruction. The Roman governor quieted his conscience by a feeble attempt to turn the attention of the mad pursuers of Jesus to another object. This failed, and "the man of sorrow" was brought forth.

Before he was led to execution by Pilate's order, he was taken out and scourged. "Oh, amazing sight!" exclaims Burkitt; "the great God of heaven and earth is led out and scourged

## CHRIST SCOURGED.

like a base slave. Behold, hard-hearted sinner the lashes wherewith thy Redeemer is cruelly tormented, to save thee from thine own accusing and condemning conscience, and to save thee from the rage and fury of devils to all eternity!"

Little need be added to such a commentary. A feeling heart must be sad to know that men, that beings of the human race, could be so mournfully misled. Had Jesus been a common mortal, the horrible torments to which he was subjected would have reflected disgrace on his tormentors. But the Jews were thus moved because he had declared himself to be the Son of God. This they pronounced to be horrible blasphemy. The proofs of his high mission they rejected, and with senseless, heartless rancour outrageously pursued a supposed impostor. A false religious zeal led them to act more like fiends than men. The sincere and pious follower of him who died on Calvary, in proportion as he abhors the sinful doings of the wretched men who thus tortured the Saviour of mankind, will be on his guard not to act with like unholy wrath, against those whom he knows to be in error. In all cases let them remember, Christ taught "Blessed are the merciful."

CHRIST BEARING THE CROSS

# CHRIST BEARING THE CROSS.

"And he, bearing his cross, went forth into a place called the place of a skull, which is called in the Hebrew Golgotha."—JOHN, xix. 17.

AFTER THE BIRTH OF CHRIST, 33 YEARS.

THE portion of Christ's history told in the text quoted above, has already been illustrated. From the narrative of the Saviour's last moments, as given by St. John, we gain a confirmation of what we read in St. Mark. According to the latter, however, he was relieved from this dreadful burthen. One Simon, a Cyrenian, our readers will remember, "coming from the country" was compelled to bear the load.

This slight variation in the two narratives is of little account. The rancorous hate of which Jesus was the object, did not subside till he was cold in death. If the Cyrenian was made to carry that which the Saviour had previously borne, we may be assured the change was not ordered with a view to spare the divine sufferer. He was only relieved from the weight of the cross through apprehension that it would exhaust his powers of endurance, before he reached the place of execution: through fear that his

## CHRIST BEARING THE CROSS.

enemies would not have the gratification of seeing him nailed to the fatal tree.

A learned minister, who has already been quoted more than once, remarks on this subject, "It was a custom among the Romans to cause the person condemned to crucifying, to carry his own cross; accordingly our Saviour bore his own cross part of the way, till fainting under the burden of it they laid it on another, not out of mercy but malice; reserving him for a more public death, they were loath he should go off in a fainting fit." The same writer supposes Christ might have sunk beneath the weight, from the cross on which he was to die being of extraordinary weight, proportionable to the crimes with which he was charged.

When Christians contemplate the awful sufferings which Jesus was doomed to know, they will learn to bear with fortitude the comparatively slight burdens which in common life are cast upon them. Remembering Him who died for them, let each rejoice that he is so largely spared, and stretching out a helping hand to a brother, sing

"Let us bear each other's load,
Faithful to each other prove;
Till we gain the Saints' abode,
Till we take our place above.

CHRIST ON THE CROSS.

## CHRIST ON THE CROSS.

"They crucified him, and two others with him, on either side one, and Jesus in the midst."—JOHN, xix. 18.

AFTER THE BIRTH OF CHRIST, 33 YEARS.

THE evangelist John now places on record the last dread scene of the Saviour's life. To fulfil an ancient prophecy, "and he was numbered with the transgressors," the great reformer Jesus, the Son of God, is seen crucified between two thieves.

Pontius Pilate wrote a title which was placed on the cross. It was written in three languages, in Hebrew, Greek, and Latin, and it ran thus: "Jesus of Nazareth, King of the Jews." The paper was read by many, as the place of execution on mount Calvary was nigh to the city. It was the custom of the Romans when a malefactor was crucified, to affix a description of the crime for which he had been doomed to die on the fatal tree. In conformity with this, Pilate caused the inscription to appear which has been quoted above. When it was read by the chief priests of the Jews, they were disposed to complain of it as incorrect, and addressing themselves to Pilate, said, "Write not, the king of the Jews;" but that "he said I am king of the Jews." They considered it would cast dishonour on the Jewish nation if it went forth to the world that such was really his quality.

The application of the chief priests proved of no avail. The Roman governor was not accustomed to such criticism, and he seems haughtily to have answered the complaint by saying, "What I have written, I have written."

The writing, which in ordinary cases was made to publish crime more largely, was in this case deemed honourable to the sufferer, and the incident is supposed by some commentators to have been specially ordained by Divine Providence. Pilate, weak and irresolute before, and easily persuaded to act against his own feelings and judgment, was here found firm and determined, and hence the inference has been drawn that it was nothing less than "the God of spirits moving upon his spirit," which caused him to write as he did, and to defend what he had written.

THE DEAD CHRIST

# THE DEAD CHRIST.

"Then the soldiers, when they had crucified Jesus, took his garments, and made four parts, to every soldier a part; and also his coat: now the coat was without seam, woven from the top throughout."—JOHN, xix 23.

AFTER THE BIRTH OF CHRIST, 33 YEARS.

BEFORE the Saviour of mankind underwent his last fearful punishment, the soldiers stripped him of his garments, which garments they divided among them, with the exception of his coat, which being "without seam, woven from the top throughout, could not be easily divided. For this, therefore, they cast lots, and thus fulfilled, we may be assured without knowing it, the Scripture prophecy found in the twenty-second Psalm: "They part my garments among them, and cast lots for my vesture."

Joseph of Arimathæa, having obtained permission to bury Jesus, the *Dead Christ* was removed from the cross. Joseph in this work of charity was assisted by Nicodemus, who had formerly visited Jesus. He brought with him "a mixture of myrrh and aloes about an hundred pound weight."

Of the treatment of the Saviour's remains notice has already been taken in "The En-

## THE DEAD CHRIST.

tombment of Jesus," but every thing connected with his name is of such interest that the account of the funeral of Christ, furnished by St. John, ought not to be omitted. In his gospel we read, "Then took they the body of Jesus and wound it in linen clothes with the spices, as the manner of the Jews is to bury. Now in the place where he was crucified there was a garden; and in the garden a new sepulchre, wherein was never man yet laid. There laid they Jesus therefore, because of the Jews' preparation day, for the sepulchre was nigh at hand."

This account will be found in substance the same as the former one, but here it is not mentioned that the tomb belonged to Joseph of Arimathæa. A napkin was put about Christ's head, and linen grave-clothes were provided, as we find in a subsequent chapter. The liberality of Joseph, assisted as he was by Nicodemus, supplied all that was deemed fitting for the last resting-place of a departed mortal.

MARY MAGDALENE AND THE DISCIPLES

# MARY MAGDALENE AND THE DISCIPLES.

"The first day of the week cometh Mary Magdalene early, when it was yet dark, unto the sepulchre, and seeth the stone taken away from the sepulchre."—JOHN, xx. 1.

AFTER THE BIRTH OF CHRIST, 33 YEARS.

CHRIST suffered on Friday. On the next day, which was the Sabbath of the Jews, Mary Magdalene did not seek the tomb of Jesus, but early on the first day of the week, she repaired to it, and soon discovered that the corpse was there no longer. "Then," writes St. John, "she runneth and cometh to Simon Peter, and to the other disciple whom Jesus loved, and saith unto them, They have taken away the Lord out of the sepulchre, and we know not where they have laid him." Whatever the love and admiration which she had felt for Christ while living, she was not prepared for that which had now come to pass, and missing the body which had been there deposited, she concluded that it had been borne to some less honourable grave.

On hearing her report, Peter and the other disciple ran to satisfy themselves of the real state of the case. Peter was outrun, and the

## MARY MAGDALENE AND THE DISCIPLES.

other disciple stooping, and looking in, saw the linen clothes in which the body had been wrapped, lying; but he did not enter the tomb. Peter then coming up went in, and saw also the linen clothes and the napkin that had been put about the head of Christ.

The disciples retired, but Mary remained at the sepulchre weeping, when suddenly she saw "two angels in white sitting, the one at the head and the other at the feet, where the body of Jesus had lain." They inquired of her why she wept, and she replied, "Because they have taken away my Lord, and I know not where they have laid him." Then turning back she saw Jesus, but knew him not. To him she repeated her complaint, and begged to know where the corpse had been carried that she might take it away. In the next moment her grief was dispelled, for Christ spoke to her and she recognised him. "Touch me not," he said, "for I am not yet ascended to my Father: but go to my brethren, and say unto them, I ascend unto my Father, and your Father; and to my God, and your God."

Great must have been her surprise, unspeakable her joy, at thus finding the Lord had arisen from the dead.

CHRIST APPEARING TO MARY MAGDALENE.

# CHRIST APPEARING TO MARY MAGDALENE.

"Jesus saith unto her, woman, why weepest thou? whom seekest thou? She, supposing him to be the gardener, saith unto him, Sir, if thou hast borne him hence, tell me where thou hast laid him, and I will take him away."—JOHN, chap. xx., verse 15.

AFTER THE BIRTH OF CHRIST, 33 YEARS.

WHEN Mary had discovered the angels who were in the sepulchre in which the form of the crucified Jesus had been deposited, it has been seen she wept, and the cause of her weeping she explained to them was, that his corpse had been removed. Her grief was not abated even though she saw Him restored to life. This may seem strange, but when it was the divine pleasure that the Son of God should assume human form, it doubtless gave the Lord power and authority to vary that form, when, for wise purposes, it might be requisite.

In more than one instance we find this power was exercised. On several occasions Christ appeared to those with whom he had been most familiar, yet was not recognised. Mary, even when spoken to by Jesus, knew him not. He marked her tearful countenance, and addressed her in the language of kindness, saying—"Woman, why weepest thou? Whom seekest thou?" Still she knew him not. His form did not give conviction to her eye; his voice was not acknowledged by her ear. Far from supposing she was admitted to the privilege of conversing with the Lord, she believed him to be only the gardener, and entreated him, if he had carried away the body, to make her acquainted with the spot to which it had been borne, that she might transfer it to a more seemly resting-place.

It has been seen that her perplexity was of short duration. Jesus uttered her name. At the word "Mary," she "turned herself, and saith unto him, Rabboni, which is to say master."

The disconsolate state of Mary at discovering that the body of Jesus was not where she expected it would be found, may be likened to the grief and embarrassment which many faint-hearted Christians experience, while seeking to know him in the spirit.

If such the distressing annoyances which sometimes beset the Christian's path, holy hope suggests that they shall not endure for ever; that those who, like Mary, "seek shall find," and in the end rejoice that their anxious cares have not been in vain.

THE INCREDULITY OF THOMAS

# THE INCREDULITY OF THOMAS.

"Jesus saith unto him, Thomas because thou hast seen me, thou hast believed: blessed are they that have not seen, and yet have believed."—JOHN, chap. xx., verse 29.

AFTER THE BIRTH OF CHRIST, 33 YEARS.

THE resurrection of Christ from the grave, was an event so wonderful, that those who reported it were not believed, and were in many instances derided for being imposed upon by tales which scoffers treated with contempt.

Good people have not unfrequently been disturbed in their faith by the idle ridicule levelled at sacred truths. Such was probably the case with Thomas, called Didymus. He was one of the twelve, but was not with his brethren, when Jesus, risen from the grave, came to them. Though the other disciples reported to him that they had seen the Lord, he could not be satisfied that they had spoken the truth, and said, "Except I shall see in his hands the print of the nails, and thrust my hand into his side, I will not believe."

Eight days after this had passed, the disciples were again assembled, and Thomas was among them. The doors of the building in which they met being shut, Jesus again ap-

## THE INCREDULITY OF THOMAS.

peared, and standing in the midst of them, greeted his former companions with the blessed words, "Peace be unto you."

All must have been astonished at this new visit, and more so still when he intimated that he was aware of what the incredulous disciple had declared. To him he especially addressed his speech. "Thomas, reach hither thy finger, and behold my hands; and reach hither thy hand, and thrust it into my side: and be not faithless, but believing."

The proof thus offered was all-convincing; the doubts of Thomas were no more, and in amazement and penitence he could only answer, "My Lord, and my God."

Jesus then said to him, "Thomas, because thou hast seen me, thou hast believed; blessed are they that have not seen, and yet have believed."

To believe only what we can look upon, in the ordinary affairs of life would be folly, would be madness. What presumption would it be to withhold belief in Christ because we had not seen him with our mortal eyes! This would be to require him to return to the world so often as weak men might choose to dispute that evidence which had been pronounced indisputable by millions of our forefathers.

THE GREAT DRAUGHT OF FISHES.

# THE GREAT DRAUGHT OF FISHES.

"He said unto them, cast the net on the right side of the ship, and ye shall find. They cast therefore, and now they were not able to draw it for the multitude of fishes."—JOHN, chap. xxi., verse 6.

---

AFTER THE BIRTH OF CHRIST, 33 YEARS.

---

THE draught of fishes of which John here writes, is not to be confounded with that already illustrated, as recorded in the gospel of St. Luke. The miraculous draught of fishes spoken of by Luke occurred at an early period of the ministry of our Lord, and then it was that Simon Peter and his companions were appointed to be "fishers of men."

That of which John tells, was witnessed after Christ had completed the great work which he came to perform; had been crucified, and his lifeless form deposited in the grave.

The disciples went in a ship to fish, but toiled all night in vain. When the morning returned they perceived Jesus standing on the shore, but the disciples not expecting to meet him there, did not know him. He then addressed them, saying, "Children have ye any meat?" They were obliged to answer "No;"

## THE GREAT DRAUGHT OF FISHES.

and he then directed them how to throw their net, and though they had taken nothing before, now they secured so many, that "they were not able to draw it (the net) for the multitude of fishes." Thus it was that the disciples knew by whom they had been guided to the great benefit which had so unexpectedly cheered them, after many hours of fruitless toil.

In thus presenting himself at such a moment, and with such happy effect, we may perceive that Christ is not unmindful of the temporal wants of his followers. He knew the wants of the disciples, and he knew how to relieve them. A learned divine, writing on this passage of the Redeemer's wondrous story, remarks, "Christ our mediator is true God, and as such he has a sovereign power and providence over all the creatures; the cattle on a thousand hills, and all the fish swimming in the sea, are obedient to his power and observant to his command."

If we are careful to remember that with boundless power the Saviour unites love and pity for men in the mortal state, more will not be wanting to save the feeble Christian from yielding to despondency.

CHRIST'S CHARGE TO PETER

# CHRIST'S CHARGE TO PETER.

"So when they had dined, Jesus saith to Simon Peter, Simon, son of Jonas, lovest thou me more than these? He saith unto him, yea, Lord; thou knowest that I love thee. He saith unto him, feed my lambs."—JOHN, chap. xxi., verse 15.

AFTER THE BIRTH OF CHRIST, 33 YEARS.

AFTER the disciples had been cheered by the miraculous draught of fishes, Jesus dined with them, and when the repast was over, he enquired of Simon Peter, "if he loved him more than his fellows did?" and when Peter replied, "Yea, Lord, thou knowest I love thee." Christ gave him this charge, "Feed my sheep." A second time he put the same question, and receiving a like answer, he repeated the charge, "Feed my sheep."

John then writes, "He saith unto him the third time, Simon, son of Jonas, lovest thou me? Peter was grieved because he said unto him the third time, lovest thou me? And he said unto him, Lord, thou knowest all things; thou knowest that I love thee. Jesus said unto him, Feed my sheep."

There is much to note in this remarkable verse. Peter is hurt that the same question should be put to him thrice. It doubtless

## CHRIST'S CHARGE TO PETER.

reminded him that thrice he had denied that he was one of Christ's followers; having previously declared, "Though all men forsake thee, yet will not I." He no longer manifests the same confidence in himself which he formerly possessed; he no longer presumes to exalt himself above all men. To the question, "Lovest thou me more than these?" he humbly replies, "Lord, thou knowest all things, thou knowest I love thee."

His humility is rewarded. "Jesus saith unto him, Feed my sheep." Appointed by the Redeemer to watch over the welfare of those for whom he had left his native heaven to live in poverty on earth, and die a horrible death, he appointed him to feed the sheep of "the Good Shepherd;" Peter must have greatly rejoiced. All misgivings growing out of his former weakness were of course removed, when Christ, assured of his love, conferred upon him this honour, and gave him so important a charge; so holy and honourable a post.

CHRIST PREPARING THE APOSTLES.

# CHRIST PREPARING THE APOSTLES.

"And, being assembled together with them, commanded them that they should not depart from Jerusalem, but wait for the promise of the Father, which, saith he, ye have heard of me."—ACTS, chap. i., verse 4.

AFTER THE BIRTH OF CHRIST, 33 YEARS.

THE book called "The Acts of the Apostles" contains many facts which are not to be found in the four Gospels. It also presents many edifying lessons, by the careful perusal of which the young and the old, the rich and the poor, all classes of men, may be largely benefitted.

In the first chapter we have a most valuable record of the doings of Jesus, after he had reappeared from the grave. It was important, for the future well-being of mankind, that infallible proof should be supplied of his having risen from the dead, and he therefore suffered himself to be seen during forty days by many. The disciples being assembled he joined them, and commanded them not to depart from Jerusalem, but wait for the promise of the Father, which he reminded them they had heard of from him, for "John truly baptised with water," but those to whom his speech was addressed, he now declared should be baptised with the Holy Ghost.

The disciples expected that the temporal greatness of Israel might be revived, and they asked, "Lord, wilt thou at this time restore the kingdom to Israel?" He answered, "It is not for you to know the times or the seasons which the Father hath put in his own power."

The Lord then declared that his followers should "receive power after the Holy Ghost had come upon them, and they should be witnesses to him both in Jerusalem, and in all Judea and Samaria, and unto the uttermost parts of the earth."

When Christ had spoken thus he rose from the earth and passed into a cloud, which veiled him from their sight. They looked, and while thus engaged two men stood by them in white apparel, men in form, but it may be presumed angels in reality, who said to them, "Men of Galilee, why stand ye gazing up into heaven? This same Jesus, which is taken up from you into heaven, shall so come in like manner as ye have seen him go into heaven."

Grand and extraordinary as the spectacle was which they had been permitted to behold, still more glorious was the prophecy or promise thus held out to believers in the Saviour.

DESCENT OF THE HOLY GHOST.

# DESCENT OF THE HOLY GHOST.

"And suddenly there came a sound from heaven as of a rushing mighty wind, and it filled all the house where they were sitting."—ACTS, chap. ii., verse 2.

AFTER THE BIRTH OF CHRIST, 34 YEARS.

FIFTY days had passed since the resurrection of Jesus from the grave, and the apostles, whom he had repeatedly visited within that period, now applied themselves with earnestness to make the name and the doctrine of their master known. They prayed to the Lord, who knew the hearts of all men, that he would direct them in their choice of those who might be associated in their labours. Looking at the vast field over which those labours were to extend, it naturally occurred to them that there would be some difficulty in finding men duly accomplished, to preach in other lands the word of God in a language not then known to them. On this subject they were deliberating, when one of the mightiest miracles on record was graciously vouchsafed from above, to relieve them from their embarrassment.

It was in that hour that the Holy Ghost descended upon them. They were all assembled when there came a sound, an awful sound,

## DESCENT OF THE HOLY GHOST.

as of a rushing mighty wind, which "filled all the house" in which they were sitting; and filled its inmates with wonder. They had not recovered from the astonishment which this caused them to experience, when their wondering eyes beheld "cloven tongues as of fire," which came "and sat on each of them!"

If this sight was enough to awaken surprise and admiration, with equal gratitude and amazement must they have contemplated that which immediately followed. From that hour the servants of the Saviour received "the gift of tongues;" that is, men unlearned before, or knowing only the language of the country in which they had lived, found themselves, "as the Spirit gave them utterance," competent to address men of other lands in their own tongue.

It was in this way, that the great obstacles which had opposed the first ministers of Christ were there removed. Thus educated or inspired, hope naturally took place of doubt and dismay, and the disciples were prepared to go forth on their heavenly mission, "conquering and to conquer."

ST PETER'S FIRST SERMON IN JERUSALEM.

# ST. PETER'S FIRST SERMON IN JERUSALEM.

"But Peter, standing up with the eleven, lifted up his voice, and said unto them, Ye men of Judea, and all ye that dwell at Jerusalem, be this known unto you, and hearken to my words."—ACTS, chap. ii., verse 14.

AFTER THE BIRTH OF CHRIST, 35 YEARS.

THE powers with which the disciples of Jesus were suddenly invested caused them to be listened to with great amazement. It was no common thing for the same individuals, and those not men of great learning, but taken from the humblest, least educated classes of society, to be able to speak to Parthians, Medes, Elamites, Mesopotamians, Cappadocians, Pamphilians, and others, in their own languages. Some who heard them were properly moved at hearing them discourse of the wonderful works of God, but others indulged in idle mockery, and said of the gifted followers of the Lord, "These men are full of new wine."

Then it was that Peter preached his first sermon in Jerusalem. Standing with the eleven, he lifted up his voice and said to them, "Ye men of Judea, and all ye that dwell at Jerusalem, be this known unto you, and hearken to

## ST. PETER'S FIRST SERMON IN JERUSALEM.

my words. For these are not drunken, as ye suppose, seeing it is but the third hour of the day, but this is that which was spoken by the prophet Joel, "And it shall come to pass in the last days, I will pour out of my spirit upon all flesh; and your sons and your daughters shall prophesy, and your young men shall see visions, and your old men shall dream dreams. And on my servants and on my hand-maidens I will pour out in those days of my spirit, and they shall prophecy; and I will show wonders in heaven above, and signs in the earth beneath; blood and fire, and vapour of smoke. The sun shall be turned into darkness, and the moon into blood, before that great and notable day of the Lord come."

The apostle Peter, endowed with prophetic foresight, announces changes most appalling to behold, which are to precede the great day; but how consoling is the assurance that follows, how important to be constantly borne in mind, that "whoever shall call on the name of the Lord shall be saved!"

PETER AND JOHN CURING THE LAME MAN

# PETER AND JOHN CURING THE LAME MAN.

"And he took him by the right hand, and lifted him up: and immediately his feet and ancle bones received strength."—ACTS, chap iii., verse 7.

AFTER THE BIRTH OF CHRIST, 35 YEARS.

PETER and John, remaining in Jerusalem, went one day to the Temple at the hour of prayer, when a poor man, who had been lame all his life, was carried to the gate which was called 'Beautiful,' to ask alms of those who resorted thither. On his supplicating John and Peter, the latter told the man to look on them, and when he did so in the hope of receiving some small gift, Peter thus addressed him: "Silver and gold have I none, but such as I have I give thee." He added, "In the name of Jesus Christ of Nazareth, rise up and walk."

With these words he took the cripple by the right hand and lifted him up, and "immediately his feet and ankle bones received strength."

The poor man was wholly relieved from his infirmity; was completely cured. He stood, he walked, he even leaped! He entered the Temple with those who had conferred on him this

## PETER AND JOHN CURING THE LAME MAN.

unhoped-for benefit, praising God for his mercy.

Crowds of people saw the man so miraculously restored. They followed to look at him, when Peter thought it right to declare to them, that it was not by the holiness or power of himself and John, that what they saw had been effected. "It is," said he, at once admonishing and rebuking those about him, "It is the God of Abraham, and of Isaac, and of Jacob, the God of our fathers hath glorified his son Jesus; that Jesus whom ye delivered up, and denied him in the presence of Pilate, when he was determined to let him go, that has enabled this man to walk." He reminded them that they had spared a murderer while they crucified Christ. Though they killed the Prince of Life, God had raised him from the dead, as he and his companion could witness, and now it was his influence that commanded their admiration, as it was faith in his holy name, that gave him the comfort in which he then rejoiced, and for which, as became him, he was returning thanks to the Almighty.

PETER BEFORE THE HIGH PRIEST.

# PETER BEFORE THE HIGH PRIEST.

"And when they had set him in the midst, they asked, by what power, or by what name, have ye done this?"—ACTS, chap. iv., verse 7.

AFTER THE BIRTH OF CHRIST, 35 YEARS.

WHEN the lame man had been cured at the gate of the temple called "the Beautiful," Peter addressed those who were by. He stated the miracle to have been wrought not by any power that he and John possessed of themselves, but by the goodness of God, who had sent to them his Son Jesus, whom they had crucified. Some who heard his words were not pleased at being reminded of their past misdeeds. They reported what had been told to the people, and in consequence the captains of the temple, and the Sadducees "laid hands upon them, and put them in hold unto the next day." The Sadducees were grieved at hearing the apostles preach the resurrection of the dead through Jesus Christ, as many who heard the word believed.

The servants of the Lord remained unmoved, by the angry feelings which were arrayed against them. They lifted up their voices with one accord, saying, "Lord, thou art God, which hast made heaven, and earth, and the sea, and all that in them is: who, by the mouth of thy servant David hast said, Why did the heathen rage, and the people imagine vain things?" They called on God to "behold the threatenings" opposed to them, and to grant to them "that with all boldness they might speak his word, by stretching forth his hand to heal, and that signs and wonders might be done by the holy name of Jesus."

After they had thus prayed, a new miracle was witnessed. The place in which they were was shaken, and they were filled with the Holy Ghost. The multitude assembled believed; they were of one heart, and many who were the possessors of houses and lands sold them and laid the price of them at the apostles' feet.

Such, in that important hour, was shewn to be the efficacy of prayer, and such the power which God conferred on his servants who boldly preached in the name of Jesus Christ.

THE DEATH OF ANANIAS.

# THE DEATH OF ANANIAS.

"And Ananias hearing these words fell down, and gave up the ghost: and great fear came on all them that heard these things."—ACTS, chap. v., verse 5.

AFTER THE BIRTH OF CHRIST, 35 YEARS.

IN numerous instances the Scriptures teach us to admire the mercy of God, but they also show us the awful judgments with which he visits sin.

Such a lesson is brought before us in the sad case of Ananias. He was among those who sold their land, and laid the price of it at the apostles' feet. But Ananias was not sincere. Pretending to offer the whole, he only gave a part of what he had received.

The falsehood became known to Peter, who thereupon solemnly reproved the dissembler. "Why," he asked, "hath Satan filled thine heart to lie to the Holy Ghost, and keep back part of the price of the land? Whilst it remained was it not thine own? and after it was sold was it not in thine own power? Why hast thou conceived this thing in thine heart? Thou hast not lied unto men, but unto God."

Mark what followed. Ananias heard these

words. He knew that he had sought to appear what he was not, and the next moment he fell dead!

Great fear came upon all who heard of his fate. Hypocrisy is a crying sin. A wretched man, we see, falsely gives out that, filled with the Holy Ghost, he is prepared to resign all he possesses to the servants of the Lord, yet artfully keeps back a part. He was not required to give to them, but affecting great piety, shamming unbounded zeal, he made a vain display that among men he might appear indifferent to wealth, and only anxious to promote the best interests of religion. For this wicked exercise of his cunning, he was instantly struck dead.

The young and the old who read this fearful story with due attention, will tremble at the bare thought of uttering a falsehood; for God cannot be deceived, he "is a Spirit that must be worshipped in spirit and in truth."

THE DEATH OF SAPPHIRA.

# THE DEATH OF SAPPHIRA.

"Then fell she down straightway at his feet, and yielded up the ghost: and the young men came in, and found her dead, and, carrying her forth, buried her by her husband."—Acts, chap. v., verse 10.

### AFTER THE BIRTH OF CHRIST, 35 YEARS.

When Ananias had breathed his last, the young men whose business it was to bury the dead came in, enveloped his remains in a winding-sheet, and carried him to his grave.

His wife Sapphira was not present when he ventured on that deceit which had proved fatal to the unhappy man. About three hours afterwards she returned, and entering the place in which the apostles were, was questioned by Peter as to the price of the land which had been sold. Sapphira knew nothing of what had befallen her husband, but was no doubt aware of the false report, which he had made up his mind to impose upon those who preached in the name of Jesus.

Peter now said to her, speaking in reference to what Ananias had stated, "Tell me whether ye sold the land for so much? And she said, Yea, for so much. Then Peter said unto her, How is it that ye have agreed together to tempt the

## THE DEATH OF SAPPHIRA.

spirit of the Lord? Behold, the feet of them that have buried thy husband are at the door, and shall carry thee out. Then fell she down straightway at his feet, and yielded up the ghost."

It is difficult to imagine anything more thrilling than the words which Peter found himself called upon to address to the artful Sapphira. She supposed her husband still living, and that it was impossible to detect the falsehood she uttered. The next moment she was undeceived, told her husband was no more, and that her own death was at hand.

This is the only instance in the New Testament in which such severe punishment was brought on any offenders by the apostles. It was to work good, to warn all who might read or hear of it against sham piety.

THE STONING OF ST STEPHEN.

# THE STONING OF ST. STEPHEN

"And he kneeled down, and cried with a loud voice, Lord lay not this sin to their charge. And when he had said this he fell asleep."—ACTS, chap. vii., verse 60.

AFTER THE BIRTH OF CHRIST, 35 YEARS.

SAINT STEPHEN was one of those pious men who was chosen as full of faith and of the Holy Ghost, who devoted themselves continually to prayer and to the word, and who was empowered to perform great miracles. He preached with such power, that those who wished to oppose his doctrine could not answer his arguments. The elders and scribes then brought him before the council, charged with having said, "Jesus of Nazareth should destroy that place."

Unawed by all that men could urge against him, his face, while he was before the council, was seen "as if it had been the face of an angel." He answered his accusers by describing what God had done for Israel, and by telling them of their fathers' sinful conduct and their own. These things cut them to the heart. They gnashed their teeth. Still fearless, and full of the Holy Ghost, Stephen looked up stedfastly into heaven, and saw the glory of

## THE STONING OF ST. STEPHEN.

God, and Jesus standing on the right hand of the Almighty.

Upon this those who heard him stopped their ears, cast him out of the city, and stoned him to death. "The witnesses laid down their clothes at a young man's feet, whose name was Saul. While being stoned, Stephen called out aloud, Lord Jesus receive my spirit." We farther read that he kneeled down, and cried with a loud voice, "Lord, lay not this sin to their charge. And when he had said this he fell asleep."

To him whose conscience is pure, heaven seems to open in his last hour, and he feels that "to die is gain."

THE CONVERSION OF SAUL.

# THE CONVERSION OF SAUL.

"And he fell to the earth, and heard a voice saying unto him, Saul, Saul, why persecutest thou me?"—ACTS, chap. ix., verse iv.

AFTER THE BIRTH OF CHRIST, 36 YEARS.

SAUL, the young man at whose feet those concerned in the death of St. Stephen laid their clothes, approved of that barbarous deed. A spirit of persecution was then abroad, and Saul was very active in pursuing those who taught, or who favoured the gospel of Christ. He is spoken of as one "who made havoc of the church, haling men and women," and committing them to prison.

His ardour in the cause was such, that "breathing out threatenings and slaughter against the disciples," he went to the High Priest, and asked to be provided with letters to Damascus, authorising him if he found any men and women on the way, who believed in the name of Jesus, to bring them bound to Jerusalem.

Journeying with this wicked purpose, suddenly a great light shone around him from heaven. It was so insufferably bright that he instantly fell to the ground, while these words

## THE CONVERSION OF SAUL.

sounded in his ears, "Saul, Saul, why persecutest thou me?"

He trembled, as well he might, at this astounding manifestation of Divine wrath, and imploringly asked, "Lord, what wilt thou have me do?" The voice, which was that of the Lord, commanded him to go into the city, and he should be directed what course to take. He rose from the ground, but could see no one. His blindness was such that he was led into Damascus. Three days he remained in this state, during which he could neither eat nor drink.

This young man was thus awfully arrested in a career of crime. In the sequel it will be seen that the dread visitation was not only to save those whose destruction he sought, but was ordered in mercy to the sinner himself. Many, thoughtless as he was, would have everlasting reason to rejoice, if happily they might be stayed from evil, and awoke in time to a sense of their misdeeds.

SAUL RESTORED TO SIGHT.

## SAUL RESTORED TO SIGHT.

"And Ananias went his way, and entered into the house; and putting his hands on him said, Brother Saul, the Lord, even Jesus, that appeared unto thee in the way as thou camest, hath sent me, that thou mightest receive thy sight, and be filled with the Holy Ghost."—Acts, chap. ix., verse 17.

AFTER THE BIRTH OF CHRIST, 36 YEARS.

THERE lived in Damascus a disciple whose name was Ananias. The Lord appeared to him in a vision, and commanded him to go to a certain street, and there inquire "in the house of Judas, for one Saul of Tarsus." For, the Lord added, "behold, he prayeth. And hath seen in a vision a man named Ananias coming in, and putting his hand on him, that he might receive his sight.

Ananias was assured that Saul was a chosen vessel, to bear the name of the Lord before the Gentiles, and kings, and children of Israel. Entering Damascus he found the house in which the stricken persecutor was lodged, and thus addressed him, "Brother Saul, the Lord, even Jesus, that appeared unto thee in the way as thou camest, hath sent me, that thou mightest receive thy sight, and be filled with the Holy Ghost."

## SAUL RESTORED TO SIGHT.

No sooner had Saul been told this, than the scales fell from his eyes, his sight returned, he arose, and was baptized. After this he recovered his strength, and remained with the disciples in Damascus; he soon began to preach in the synagogues that Christ was the son of God.

Those who had lately been his friends became his foes. The Jews watched the gates night and day to kill him, but the other disciples saved him by letting him down in the night, over the wall of the city, in a basket.

Saul having been miraculously snatched from sin, was thus preserved from danger. "The wisdom of God," as Burkitt remarks, "is never at a loss to find out ways and means for the deliverance of his servants." For Saul, who was thus preserved, he had determined that a great, and most important labour should rest on his shoulders. Saving him was saving one, who was to benefit, by his future exertions, millions then unborn.

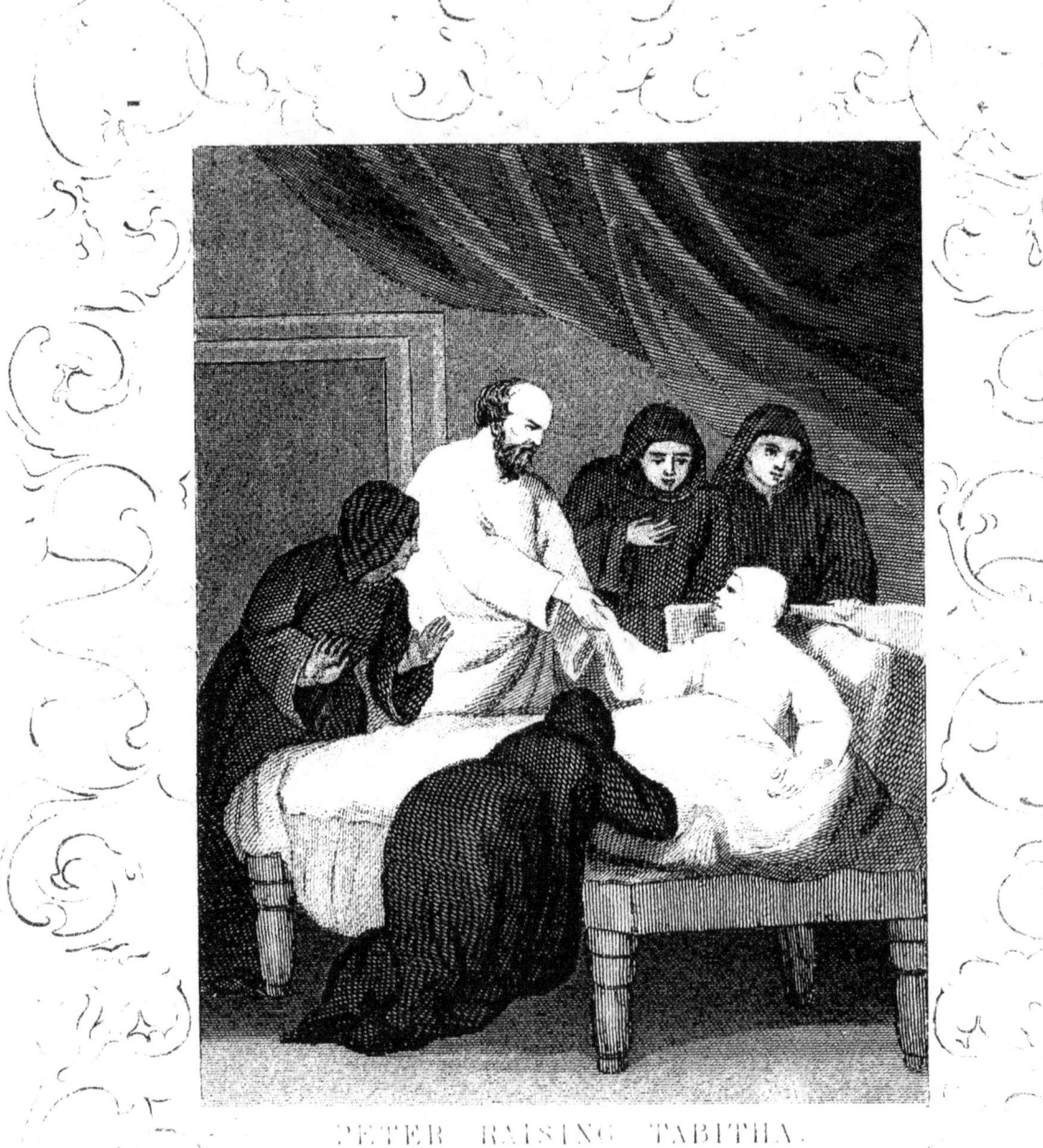

PETER RAISING TABITHA.

# PETER RAISING TABITHA.

"But Peter put them all forth, and kneeled down, and prayed; and turning him to the body said, Tabitha arise. And she opened her eyes: and when she saw Peter, she sat up."—Acts, chap. ix., verse 40.

AFTER THE BIRTH OF CHRIST, 40 YEARS.

In the city of Joppa there dwelt a holy woman, who was called one of the disciples, and whose name was Tabitha, which is considered the same as Dorcas. This Dorcas was full of good works and alms-deeds, but to the grief of the widows and other poor people, whom she had been in the habit of relieving from time to time, she died. Being dead, she was washed, and laid out in an upper chamber, preparatory to her funeral. Peter on this occasion was sent for. He was then at Lydda, which was not far from Joppa, and on being told that Dorcas was no more, he returned with the men who had brought him the sad news, and entering the chamber in which the dead body had been laid, found those whom living she had befriended, weeping for her departure, and shewing each other the coats and garments which she had made. Peter, no doubt, sympathised with the mourners, but he directed them all to withdraw, and to leave him alone with their deceased benefactress.

They left the chamber, and Peter kneeling, then prayed to that Great Being, "in whose hands are the issues of life and death," that if it stood with his high pleasure, the grief of those who then sorrowed near him might be abated. While he prayed he seems to have felt assured that his petition would be granted, and turning to the body he said, "Tabitha, arise."

These words had scarcely been spoken when she opened her eyes, and Peter then presented her to the widows and others who were in the house, restored to life and health.

Such wonders were given to the disciples to perform, that the beholders might have faith in the name of Jesus. This effect immediately followed, "and many believed in the Lord." They were duly informed that it was God alone, who, called upon in the name of his Son, thus miraculously aided those who laboured in his cause.

THE ANGEL APPEARING TO CORNELIUS.

# THE ANGEL APPEARING TO CORNELIUS.

"He saw in a vision evidently about the ninth hour of the day an angel of God coming in to him, and saying unto him, Cornelius."—ACTS, chap. x., verse 3.

AFTER THE BIRTH OF CHRIST, 40 YEARS.

CORNELIUS, an officer in the Roman army, a centurion in "the Italian band," resided in Cæsarea. He was a good man; he was devout, spent much of his time in prayer, and relieved many by giving alms.

It is recorded of him that one day he had an extraordinary vision. An angel of God came in to him, and called him by his name. Cornelius felt alarmed at this unlooked for visit, and inquired the object of it, when the angel told him that his prayers and his alms were an acceptable memorial before God, but directed him to send to Peter, who would make known to him what he ought to do.

Cornelius sent two of his household servants to Joppa to seek Peter. And when they were near their journey's end, "Peter went up upon the housetop to pray." He was hungry, but while his repast was being got ready, he fell into a trance, during which the heavens opened, and he saw a certain vessel descending unto him, as it had been a great sheet knit at the four corners, wherein were all manner of four-footed creatures, wild beasts, creeping things, and fowls of the air. And while this was before his eyes, a voice called to him, "Rise, Peter; kill, and eat." Peter then said, "Not so, Lord; for I have never eaten anything common or unclean." "What God has cleansed," the voice replied, and this was then repeated, "that call not thou unclean."

Such a vision filled Peter with amazement. It was not allowed to pass suddenly away, for we are distinctly told that it was thrice repeated.

The vessel was drawn up to heaven, and the messengers of Cornelius arrived. Their errand told, he soon consented to accompany them to Joppa. The vision presented to him had instructed him as to the course he should pursue on his arrival there.

CORNELIUS MEETING PETER.

# CORNELIUS MEETING PETER.

"And as Peter was coming in, Cornelius met him, and fell down at his feet and worshipped him."—ACTS, chap. x., verse 25.

AFTER THE BIRTH OF CHRIST, 40 YEARS.

DIRECTED by an angel to seek from Peter instruction, as to what he ought to do when Cornelius saw the disciple, who at his call had repaired to Cæsarea, "he fell down at his feet, and worshipped him."

Peter lifted him up, reminding him that he, before whom Cornelius had prostrated himself, was but a man. He then, conversing with him, remarked that it was an unlawful thing for a Jew to keep company with one of another nation, but nevertheless, God having taught him in a vision, that he ought not to "call any man common or unclean," he came to him as soon as he was sent for.

Cornelius told Peter the occasion of his sending to Joppa, remarking that he had done well to come at his invitation, as he and those who were present with him, were ready "to hear all things that were commanded him of God."

Then Peter delivered a very impressive dis-

## CORNELIUS MEETING PETER.

course, "Of a truth," said he, "I perceive that God is no respecter of persons. But in every nation he that feareth him, and worketh righteousness, is accepted with him. The word," the disciple added, "which God sent unto the children of Israel, preaching peace by Jesus Christ ye know. He is Lord of all."

Peter continuing his address, told that "God had anointed Jesus of Nazareth, who went about doing good, but who had, notwithstanding, been hanged on a tree. Jesus, however, had been raised up on the third day, had been seen by his disciples, and had eaten and drunk with them." While he was yet speaking the Holy Ghost manifested its presence, and fell on all who had heard the voice of the speaker, Gentiles as well as Jews.

From what was here witnessed, as well as from the words of the holy followers of Jesus, men are taught that "God is no respecter of persons:" but that all who fear him, and work righteousness, are acceptable in his sight. Those, whom the proud would regard as "common or unclean," and as such would deem them too humble for companionship, are, so they walk humbly before their Creator, and do their duty by their fellow-men, acceptable in the sight of the Father of all.

PETER DELIVERED OUT OF PRISON.

# PAUL DELIVERED OUT OF PRISON.

"The angel said unto him, gird thyself, and bind on thy sandals. And so he did. And he saith unto him, cast thy garment about thee, and follow me."—Acts, chap. xii., verse 8.

AFTER THE BIRTH OF CHRIST, 45 YEARS.

THE disciples experienced great persecution from a king whose name was Herod, who put James, the brother of John, to the sword, and threw Peter into prison.

He gave him into the custody of four quaternions of soldiers, intending, after Easter to bring him for some cruel purpose before the people. For this the unfortunate Peter was detained in prison.

His danger was great, his case almost hopeless, but the church of God incessantly prayed for him. Their pious exercises were not unregarded.

It was night, and on the following day Peter was to be brought forth to suffer death, or to be subjected to some monstrous indignity. Bound with two chains, trusting in God, he slept between two soldiers. The keepers watched before the door of his prison, when, "Behold,

## PAUL DELIVERED OUT OF PRISON.

the angel of the Lord came upon him, and a light shined in the prison: and he smote Peter on the side, and raised him up, saying, Arise up quickly. And his chains fell off from his hands." The angel further directed him to gird himself, put on his sandals, and follow him. Peter did so, not suspecting that he was obeying the command of a superior being. The iron gate of the building opened to give him passage, and he found himself at large in the city, and hastened to the house of Mary the mother of John. Thence he removed to a place of safety. When day returned, a great stir was made among the soldiers who had had Peter in charge. They sought for their prisoner but found him not, and Herod caused the keepers of the prison to be put to death.

The might of the wicked fails before the power of God. Chains, iron gates, and strong walls, could not detain Peter, when the angel of the Lord attended to set him free. Many of the most awful scenes recorded in the Bible attest this. Pharaoh and his host were in an instant powerless, when it was the will of the Eternal that the Red Sea should close over them.

ELYMAS THE SORCERER STRUCK BLIND.

# ELYMAS THE SORCERER.

"And now, behold, the hand of the Lord is upon thee, and thou shalt be blind, not seeing the sun for a season. And immediately there fell on him a mist and a darkness; and he went about seeking some to lead him by the hand."—Acts, chap. xiii., verse 11.

After the Birth of Christ, 45 years.

Paul and Barnabas preached the word of God in divers places, and being in the isle of Paphos, they met there with a Jew, who was a false prophet and a sorcerer. Sergius Paulus, the Roman deputy of the country, was disposed to listen to Barnabas and Paul, but in this he was opposed by Elymas the sorcerer, who sought to turn away the deputy from the faith.

Saul, who it is here mentioned was also called Paul, filled with righteous anger, fixed his gaze on the sorcerer Elymas, and thus sternly addressed him: "O full of all subtilty and all mischief, thou child of the devil, thou enemy of all righteousness, wilt thou not cease to pervert the right ways of the Lord? And now, behold, the hand of the Lord is upon thee, and thou shalt be blind, not seeing the sun for a season."

These were not mere words without meaning

## ELYMAS THE SORCERER.

and without power. Immediately after Paul had pronounced the awful sentence, a mist and darkness came over Elymas. He could not see his way from the place in which he was thus punished for his sinful daring, "and he went about seeking some to lead him by the hand."

Sergius Paulus when he saw what had befallen Elymas, was no longer to be turned from the right path by what he had said. "The deputy believed, being astonished at the doctrine of the Lord." He saw that Elymas, who had been reverenced and feared, could not for a moment resist the servant of God. The punishment which here we read fell on the sorcerer, is the more striking, seeing that he himself was one who affected to possess the gift of prophecy, and in some respects superhuman power. In his case it was seen that the authority exercised in the name of the Saviour surpassed and rendered harmless, all the unhallowed skill which impostors might pretend it was theirs to possess.

Possibly this should be regarded as a type of the total overthrow of that sophistry, which wicked men would fain oppose to the progress of gospel truth.

# PAUL AT ANTIOCH.

"But when they departed from Perga, they came to Antioch in Pisidia, and went into the synagogue on the sabbath-day, and sat down."—Acts, chap. xiii., verse 14.

AFTER THE BIRTH OF CHRIST, 46 YEARS.

Paul and his company having left Paphos, journeyed to Perga in Pamphylia, and thence proceeded to Antioch, where an interesting scene was witnessed, and a most important announcement made.

They entered the synagogue, and after the reading of the law and the prophets, which was a portion of the service appointed for the Jewish Sabbath, the rulers of the synagogue invited them, if they had any exhortation for the people to deliver it then.

Paul stood up, and having beckoned with his hand to bespeak silence and attention, he addressed the men of Israel present, and went over the principal events in Jewish history, when God choosing to exalt the forefathers of those who heard him, brought them out of the land of Egypt, and raised up David to be their king. From David's line, he added, a Saviour had been given to them in Jesus, whose coming had been foretold by John.

## PAUL AT ANTIOCH.

Then he reminded them how Jesus had been slain by the Jews, but raised from the dead, and seen by many who were witnesses of him to the people, as God would not suffer his only one to see corruption.

Through him Paul went on to say, forgiveness of sins was preached, and by him all who believed would be justified from all things from which they could not be justified by the law of Moses.

These words were attentively listened to by the Gentiles, but met with envy, contradiction, and blasphemy by the Jews. Paul and Barnabas declared, that since the latter put the word of God from them, it became their duty to turn to the Gentiles. At these happy tidings, happy for them, the Gentiles were glad, and gloried in the name of the Lord. It was soon seen that they had received extraordinary gifts from above, and they were immediately admitted to the baptismal rite.

The word, which the Jews were moved to reject with scorn, the advocates of Christianity then hastened to preach to all the world.

PAUL AND BARNABAS AT LYSTRA

# PAUL AND BARNABAS AT LYSTRA.

"Then the priest of Jupiter, which was before their city, brought oxen and garlands, unto the gates, and would have done sacrifice with the people."—ACTS, chap. xiv., verse 13.

AFTER THE BIRTH OF CHRIST, 46 YEARS.

THE wonders the apostles were enabled to perform, proved the high authority they had to teach the way to salvation, and led to some remarkable events. Paul and Barnabas having reached Lystra, saw a man who had been a cripple from his infancy, when "perceiving that he had faith to be healed," Paul said to him with a loud voice, "stand upright on thy feet," and immediately the infirmity of the beggar was no more, and he leaped and walked.

The bystanders who witnessed the astonishing change, at once concluded that Paul and his companion Barnabas were gods, who had descended to earth in the likeness of men, so familiar to the mind in those days was the idea that superior beings could appear on the earth as mortal men. Barnabas they called *Jupiter*, and Paul, *Mercury*.

It was not only the common people who

were disposed to regard the followers of Jesus as more than mortal. The priest of Jupiter brought oxen and garlands, and would have done sacrifice with the crowd, but Paul and Barnabas at this excessive homage, rent their clothes, and went among them exclaiming, "Sirs, why do ye these things? We also are men of like passions with you, and preach unto you that ye should turn from these vanities unto the living God which made heaven and earth, and the sea, and all things that are therein." Then the apostles spoke of the benefits which had been granted to men by the goodness of the Deity, and doing this, they with some difficulty restrained the people from offering sacrifice to them.

It often happens that able men perform actions that are deemed extraordinary, and are for a time almost idolised. Those who found themselves in this situation should remember the example set by Paul and Barnabas, and labour to turn men's thoughts from such vanities to fitter subjects for meditation.

PAUL STONED AT LYSTRA

# PAUL STONED AT LYSTRA.

"And there came thither certain Jews from Antioch and Iconium, who persuaded the people, and, having stoned Paul, drew him out of the city, supposing he had been dead."—ACTS, chap. xiv., verse 19.

AFTER THE BIRTH OF CHRIST, 46 YEARS.

PAUL, preaching in the name of Jesus, had taught the listeners to fix their attention on the goodness of God, who gave rain from heaven and fruitful seasons, "filling men's hearts with food and gladness." He and his companion had refused those honours which the giddy multitude were disposed to offer, supposing them to be gods, from the wonderful cure which by their means had been brought about, but after all this the people soon turned against them. Certain Jews came to Lystra from Antioch and Iconium, and in their hatred of the name of that Jesus, whom they had put to a cruel death, laboured to make those who were lately so extravagantly delighted with Paul and Barnabas, view them as wicked impostors. They so far succeeded, that Paul had nearly shared the same fate as St. Stephen. They actually stoned him, till they believed that he was dead.

## PAUL STONED AT LYSTRA.

"The devil," Dr. Burkitt remarks, "who had before laughed to see the followers of Jesus about to be adored by the Lystrians, now prompted them to murder the very men they had been disposed to exalt to the place of their idols." "He desired," that pious minister remarks, "to cause their lives to be taken away, who were seeking the destruction of his kingdom."

Paul, though supposed to have been killed, while the disciples stood about him, rose up and soon resumed his labours with industry that scorned fatigue, and zeal that knew no abatement.

That mighty Being whose servant he had become, who had in former days made known to Ananias that he was "a chosen vessel," had still important work for him to do. He was a shining light which, till his appointed task was performed, the powers of hell in vain attempted to extinguish; and it was reserved for him to preach that good men, through much tribulation, shall enter the kingdom of God

# PAUL AT PHILIPPI.

"And on the sabbath we went out of the city by a river side, where prayer was wont to be made; and we sat down, and spake unto the women which resorted thither."—Acts, chap. xvi., verse 13.

AFTER THE BIRTH OF CHRIST, 50 YEARS.

The indefatigable Paul seemed to think nothing done, till all had been effected which it was in his power to accomplish. Doubtless he felt the high importance of his mission, and this rendered him anxious to lose no time; bearing ever in his mind the solemn warning breathed by his great Preceptor, "the night cometh, in which no man can work."

Paul was at Troas, when "a vision appeared to him in the night." A man of Macedonia seemed to stand near, and "prayed him, saying, Come over into Macedonia, and help us."

In consequence of this vision, Paul and his companions concluded it was God's will that they should go to Macedonia, and preach the gospel there. They therefore left Troas for Samothracia; from that place they proceeded to Neapolis, and thence they went to Philippi, which was the chief city of one portion of Macedonia, and a colony. At Philippi, on the

## PAUL AT PHILIPPI.

sabbath-day, the disciples went out of the city by "a river side, where prayer was wont to be made." They spoke to the women who resorted thither, on sacred things, it is evident from what followed; when a certain woman, named Lydia, a seller of purple, and who came from the city of Thyatira, heard them. She worshipped God; and the Lord having opened her heart to comprehend divine truths, listened with eagerness to what fell from Paul.

Convinced of the importance of what the followers of Jesus taught, she was baptized, and all her household. Then she besought them, saying, "If ye have judged me to be faithful to the Lord, come into my house and abide there." She constrained them to avail themselves of her hospitality.

The conduct of the purple-selling woman of Thyatira sets an example which many opulent Christians ought to take shame to themselves for being slow to follow. While professing to be deeply impressed by the solemn admonitions addressed to them from the pulpit, they often evince cruel indifference to the temporal suffering of the pastor. While they own the "labourer is worthy of his hire," small as that may be, they take care that he shall receive no more.

PAUL AND SILAS IN PRISON

# PAUL AND SILAS IN PRISON.

"And when they had laid many stripes upon them, they cast them into prison, charging the jailor to keep them safely."
—Acts, chap. xvi., verse 23.

AFTER THE BIRTH OF CHRIST, 47 YEARS.

SUBSEQUENT to his narrow escape from death, Paul went to Derbe and Iconium, and even revisited Lystra. He visited other places, and being at Thyatira, a damsel came in his way, who had the reputation of being a soothsayer. She is said to have been possessed of a spirit of divination, but it was an evil spirit; and seeing Paul and his companions she followed them, saying, "These men are the servants of the most high God, which shew unto us the way of salvation."

This she repeated many days. Paul being grieved at it, said to the spirit, "I command thee in the name of Jesus Christ to come out of her." In that same hour the evil spirit left the damsel, and her powers of divination being gone, her master, who had profited from their exercise, became furious against the disciples.

In consequence of this they seized Paul and Silas, took them to the market-place, and there accused them before the rulers. The magis-

## PAUL AND SILAS IN PRISON.

trates entertained the complaint, and commanded that they should be punished with many stripes, and sent to prison.

The jailor being strictly charged to keep them safely, thrust them into the inner prison, and made their feet fast in the stocks.

In this dreary situation, Paul and his companion at midnight, sang the praises of God, when suddenly a great earthquake shook the foundations of the prison, and all the doors flew open, and every one's bands were loosed. The jailor awaking, concluded that the prisoners had escaped, and would have killed himself, but was prevented by Paul, who cried to him in a loud voice, "Do thyself no harm: for we are all here."

The jailor then called for a light, and falling before Paul and Silas, he imploringly asked, "What shall I do to be saved?" "Believe in the Lord Jesus Christ," was the answer of Paul.

That same hour he washed their stripes, he and all his house were baptized, and he then set meat before his prisoners and rejoiced, believing in God. The next day the magistrates brought them out and desired them to depart.

Thus gloriously were the servants of God saved, and their honour vindicated.

PAUL PREACHING AT EPHESUS

# PAUL PREACHING AT EPHESUS.

"He came to Ephesus, and left them there: but he himself entered into the synagogue and reasoned with the Jews."
—Acts, chap. xviii., verse 19.

AFTER THE BIRTH OF CHRIST, 48 YEARS.

Paul visited many cities. Though great the perils to which he was exposed, he was comforted and encouraged in a vision of the night, when the Lord speaking to him, said, "Be not afraid, but speak, and hold not thy peace."

At Ephesus, he entered the synagogue and reasoned with the Jews, and though he remained not long there, his labours, we have reason to believe, were not unimportant.

He seems to have allowed himself no repose. However distant the land in which he hoped the gospel might be preached with success, thither the zealous apostle directed his steps. From Ephesus he went to Cesarea, from Cesarea to Jerusalem, from Jerusalem to Antioch, and from Antioch to Galatia and Phrygia.

From the upper coasts he returned to Ephesus, where, finding certain disciples, he inquired, "Have ye received the Holy Ghost since ye believed? And they said unto him, we have not so much as heard whether there be any Holy Ghost."

Thereupon he asked unto what they had been baptized? and was answered, unto John's baptism. He told them that "John verily baptized with the baptism of repentance, saying unto the people that they should believe in him which should come after him, that is in Christ Jesus."

On hearing this, the disciples he addressed were baptized in the name of the Lord Jesus, and this being done, "when Paul had laid his hands upon them the Holy Ghost came on them." They felt themselves endowed with new powers, and prophesied. Afterwards, he entered into the synagogue, and preached and spoke boldly there.

What an example does the conduct of Paul offer to the Christian! Unbending courage, never-wearying industry, and patient perseverance, illustrate the whole of his lengthened career. In his younger days he had greatly erred. To expiate his past offences was his pious care. Few of the sons of men can deny that they have sinned, like Paul; all, like Paul, ought to repent, and atone for their misdeeds.

PAUL RESTORING LIFE TO EUTYCHUS.

# PAUL RESTORING LIFE TO EUTYCHUS.

"And Paul went down, and fell on him, and embracing him, said trouble not yourselves; for his life is in him."—ACTS, chap. xx., verse 10.

AFTER THE BIRTH OF CHRIST, 49 YEARS.

SOME of the disciples, when Paul sailed for Macedonia, were to wait for him at Troas. Those who accompanied him, with Paul, reached Phillippi, and leaving that place in five days arrived at the place where they were expected by other disciples, and there they remained a week.

On the first day of the week, Paul resumed his pious labours. Some of his brethren were to depart on the following day, and he was anxious duly to admonish and instruct them before their separation.

The disciples on this occasion were gathered together in an upper chamber, in which there were many lights. The hour at which he commenced his exhortation or sermon is not mentioned, but he continued his discourse till midnight.

There was a young man named Eutychus sat in the window of the building. He became

## PAUL RESTORING LIFE TO EUTYCHUS.

weary, while Paul continued to preach; he at length sunk into a deep sleep, and while in this state fell from the third loft, and " was taken up dead." To all, save Paul at least, it appeared that he was dead, but the apostle went to him, and embracing Eutychus, called to his parents, "Trouble not yourselves, for his life is in him."

He then broke bread with those who were present, and conversed with them, no doubt on holy things, till break of day, when Eutychus, whom they had supposed to be no more, was restored to them in health; at which they were " not a little comforted."

It will here be noted that Eutychus had nearly lost his life through giving way to sleep, while Paul was preaching in the name of Jesus. The apostle's sermon was long, but, says a pious divine, " This is not the case with our common sleepers, who at noon-day sleep under the word, nay settle and compose themselves to sleep, and do what they can to invite sleep. What, if with Eutychus, any of them fall down dead? Here is no Paul to raise them up; or what if this wretched contempt of the word provoke God to say, sleep on and be so stupified that no ordinances shall awake you: sleep on, till hell flames awake you."

PAUL BEFORE FELIX

# PAUL BEFORE FELIX.

"And as he reasoned of righteousness, temperance, and judgment to come, Felix trembled, and answered, go thy way for this time; when I have a convenient season, I will call for thee."—ACTS, chap. xxiv., verse 25.

AFTER THE BIRTH OF CHRIST, 50 YEARS.

PAUL, charged with being a "pestilent fellow, and a mover of sedition among all the Jews throughout the world," by one Tertullus, was brought before Felix, the governor of Judea, who determined to hear the case in Herod's hall.

Tertullus, who was an orator, having preferred his accusation, Paul addressed Felix. He told him that twelve days before, he had gone up to Jerusalem, to worship; but he denied that he had been found disputing with any man, or raising up the people in the synagogue, or in the city. "But," said he, "this I confess unto thee, that after the way which they call heresy, so worship I the God of my fathers, believing all things which are written in the law and in the prophets. And have hope toward God, which they themselves also allow, that there shall be a resurrection of the dead, both of the just and unjust."

## PAUL BEFORE FELIX.

"Herein," he added, "do I exercise myself, to have always a conscience void of offence toward God, and toward men." And then, describing what his conduct had been, he boldly called on his enemies to say if they had found any evil-doing in him, save that he had preached the resurrection of the dead.

Felix gave him an attentive hearing, and shewed Paul indulgence. He commanded a centurion "to keep Paul," but to let him have some liberty, and to allow "his acquaintance to minister and come to him."

Some days having passed, he caused Paul to be brought up again. The governor's wife, Drusilla, who was a Jewess, was present. The apostle then discoursed so powerfully on righteousness, temperance, and judgment to come, that Felix trembed, and said, "Go thy way for this time; when I have a convenient season I will call for thee."

Though a great impression was made on Felix, he still detained Paul, hoping to receive money from him. The words which affected him at the moment, faded from his memory. The wicked often tremble, like Felix, for their misdeeds, but like him soon forget, or disregard, the warnings they receive to change their course, and "flee from the wrath to come."

PAUL SHAKING OFF THE VIPER.

# PAUL SHAKING OFF THE VIPER.

"And he shook off the beast into the fire, and felt no harm."—Acts, chap. xxviii., verse 5.

AFTER THE BIRTH OF CHRIST, 50 YEARS.

The strange adventures of Paul were not few. He was exposed to many perils, both on the sea and on land. After the storm and shipwreck, which has been narrated, he and his companions, who had reached the shore on fragments of the vessel in which they had sailed, found themselves on an island, which was called Melita.

It seems to have been inhabited by what we call savages; a barbarous people, unacquainted with letters and the arts of civilized life. Rude as these islanders were, they showed the unfortunate persons thrown on their coast great kindness. It rained, and was cold, but they kindled a fire to cheer the strangers. Paul assisted, and having taken up a bundle of sticks, laid it on the fire, when a viper fastened on his hand.

The barbarians who were about him saw this. They knew a viper to be a most venomous reptile, whose bite or sting is usually mortal, and they said among themselves, with reference

## PAUL SHAKING OFF THE VIPER.

to what had happened to Paul, "This man is a murderer, whom, though he hath escaped the sea, yet vengeance suffereth not to live."

To their surprise, however, the apostle shook off the creature into the fire, and felt no harm.

The ignorant people of Melita had expected to see the supposed murderer suddenly swollen with the venom of the reptile; indeed they looked to see him fall dead; but, when they perceived that he had sustained no injury, "they changed their minds, and said that he was a god."

This history exhibits, in a striking point of view, the mutable character of weak ignorant men. In one instance we have seen them, after offering Paul divine honours, seeking to take away his life; in this, after suspecting the apostle to be a murderer, they are persuaded that he is a god. "Thus," says Dr. Burkitt, "upon changes of providence, many change their opinions of men; sometimes for the better, but commonly for the worse. Lord, help me only to esteem myself by the esteem which I have with thee."

THE DRAGON PERSECUTES THE WOMAN

# THE DRAGON PERSECUTING THE WOMAN.

"And there appeared a great wonder in heaven; a woman clothed with the sun, and the moon under her feet, and upon her head a crown of twelve stars."—REVELATION, chap. xii., verse 1.

"THE Revelation of St. John the Divine" is a portion of the New Testament which forcibly arrests the attention of the serious reader, as it reveals things which could only be made known to man by an inhabitant of the world above. Looking at the sublime images here presented, the student may be led to exclaim,

"Into the heaven of heavens I have presumed."

Visions of surpassing glory were vouchsafed to John. He speaks of a woman clothed with the sun, and the moon under her feet, and crowned with twelve stars. The woman is described as likely to become a mother. She suffered pain, when a great red dragon approached her. The monster had seven heads and ten horns, and seven crowns upon his heads, and his tail drew the third part of the stars of heaven, and did cast them to the earth. He stood before the woman, ready to devour her child as soon as it should be born.

## THE DRAGON PERSECUTING THE WOMAN.

John goes on to tell, that after the woman had given birth to a man-child, the dragon was foiled. It was ordained that " her child should rule all nations with a rod of iron ;" and he was " caught up unto God, and to his throne." The woman escaped into the wilderness, " where she hath a place prepared of God, that they should feed her there a thousand two hundred and threescore days."

By the woman, learned divines understand the Christian church is imaged. Being clothed in the sun, represents the church clad in righteousness. The changing moon, at her feet, images the world; the stars, her ministers—the twelve apostles. By the dragon, Satan is meant, who would fain destroy Christ. The woman being preserved in the wilderness, shews the church of Christ, though assailed by the great enemy shall be saved from his ower.

MICHAEL AND THE DRAGON

# MICHAEL AND THE DRAGON.

"And there was war in heaven: Michael and his angels fought against the dragon; and the dragon fought and his angels."— REVELATION, chap. xii., verse 7.

THE dragon, which St. John describes he saw in his vision, made war in heaven upon the angel Michael and his fellow angels. There he "prevailed not." In other words, the evil one, Satan, was defeated by the faithful servants of the Most High: "That old serpent called the Devil was cast out into the earth, and his angels were cast out with him."

By Michael and his angels, Christ is understood to be meant. He alone can overcome the great enemy of mankind. The victory so gained, Christians cannot too highly value. Sad indeed will be their case who refuse to profit by it; for, says Dr. Burkitt, "how dreadful will an imprisonment be, with devils and damned spirits, to eternal ages!—to lie for ever with Satan in that mysterious fire of hell, whose strange property it is, always to torture, but never to kill; or, always to kill, but never to consume."

We have, however, the testimony of St. John, that the victory of Michael and his angels— that is, of Christ and his ministers—was shewn to be most complete. "I heard," he says, "a loud voice saying, in heaven, Now is come salvation, and strength, and the kingdom of our God, and the power of his Christ: for the accuser of our brethren is cast down, which accused them before our God day and night. And they overcame him by the blood of the Lamb."

"Rejoice, ye heavens," he adds. But words of awful import follow: "Woe to the inhabitants of the earth, and of the sea; for the devil is come down unto you, having great wrath."

See we not, in part, the fulfilment of this prophecy? Looking at the wickedness which has prevailed, may we not conclude that the devil has been industriously at work in our world? Woe has fallen on the inhabitants of the earth; but hope suggests that joy and glory will yet be known, through the blood of the Lamb. Simple reason will not fail to suggest, what it is the province of religion to teach, that a gracious Deity will not suffer the Evil One eventually to prevail.

THE FIRST COMMANDMENT

# THE FIRST COMMANDMENT.

"Thou shalt have no other gods before me."—EXODUS, chap. xx., verse 3.

BEFORE THE BIRTH OF CHRIST, 1450 YEARS.

THE Decalogue, or the Ten Commandments, we read in the Bible, were uttered by the Almighty. God delivered them to his servant Moses, for the guidance of that favoured race, the children of Israel. They have since formed the basis of every code of laws devised for the government of men in all the more enlightened nations of the earth.

In the first commandment, the Lord declared that those whom he had brought from the land of Egypt, and delivered out of the house of bondage, should have no god but him. Then, as in later days, weak vain men existed, who could believe that masses of stone, or lumps of metal, might bless and preserve them, or who could doubt that there existed a God at all. This strange assault on revelation was of frequent occurrence. Men could not doubt their own existence, but they denied that it had an intelligent Author; they proclaimed that all things they saw were the work of chance. They maintained that "the eye, the animal to which it belonged, every plant, and every organized body, were only some of the varieties and combinations which the lapse of infinite ages had brought into existence." It has been truly answered, that to speak thus, is not less absurd than it would be to suppose, "all the implements of the cabinet-maker's workshop were substances accidentally configurated, which the artisan had converted to his use; that his adzes, saws, planes, and gimlets, were not made in order to hew, cut, smooth, shape out, or bore wood; but that these things offering themselves, the cabinet-maker saw they were fit for such purposes, and used them accordingly." It is difficult for any rational being to entertain such a supposition for a moment; but still more startling, it has been well observed, " is such a solution, if applied to those parts of animals, the action of which does not depend on the will of the animal. Is it possible to believe that the eye, as an organ of sight, resulted from such a discovery, and the animal's application of it? The well-regulated, pious mind, gazing on the wonders of creation, will feel no difficulty in recognising the existence, greatness, and bounty of a Creator—of one Lord of all.

THE SECOND COMMANDMENT

# THE SECOND COMMANDMENT.

"Thou shalt not make unto thee any graven image, or any likeness of any thing that is in heaven above, or that is in the earth beneath, or that is in the water under the earth: thou shalt not bow down thyself to them, nor serve them: for I the Lord thy God am a jealous God, visiting the iniquity of the fathers upon the children unto the third and fourth generation of them that hate me; and shewing mercy unto thousands of them that love me, and keep my commandments."—EXODUS, chap. xx., verses 4, 5, 6.

BEFORE THE BIRTH OF CHRIST, 1450 YEARS.

The second commandment contains a stern prohibition of idol worship.

When we contemplate the gross folly of a living, thinking man bending the knee to a dull unconscious piece of wood or stone, we for a moment feel astonished that such a commandment should have been necessary—that such misconduct could require to be interdicted. But such is the proneness of man to sin, that in all ages he has been found surrendering himself to this mad, abject self-abasement. In Egypt, huge masses of stone, fashioned with great care, and by many years of toil, into monstrous exaggerations, and odious caricatures of the human form, were honoured and solicited, as if they pos-

## THE SECOND COMMANDMENT.

sessed the power of bestowing health or wealth, and of inflicting punishment or death.

Not less degrading was that idolatry which could worship living creatures. Strange to say, no brute so mean—nay, more—no reptile so odious or contemptible—but some of the sons of Adam have been found to hold it sacred, and to offer senseless homage at its temple or den.

How strange is the depravity, the weakness of mortals! They can gaze on the beauties of nature, as seen in this our world—they can look on the glorious sun, and the stars of heaven, and doubt if they had a Creator; and then fix their thoughts on some despicable object, as worthy of their devout attention and boundless admiration! they can forget its obvious helplessness, and deem it omnipotent. The race of men born in Christian lands are happily spared, in our days, such extremity of degradation as was formerly known; but even now the madness is only abated, not cured. May it be ours to attune our hearts to the true God—to the author of our being, the source of every blessing, that each may now, and to the end of his days, be able to say,

"I trust in Thee, and know in whom I trust."

THE THIRD COMMANDMENT

# THE THIRD COMMANDMENT.

"Thou shalt not take the name of the Lord thy God in vain; for the Lord will not hold him guiltless that taketh his name in vain."—EXODUS, chap. xx., verse 7

Young people are often admonished to take heed how they speak of a respected fellow-creature; of a man who fills a high situation, or who has been a benefactor to this or that family. If the propriety of such restraint be acknowledged—and of its fitness none can doubt, how much more important is it, that every one should be on his guard when speaking of the mighty Creator of the world! of the Giver of all Good! not to take his name in vain!

Some have interpreted the phrase "taketh his name in vain," to have reference to a false assertion, coupled with an appeal to the Deity for its truth. Of the monstrous turpitude of such conduct, there cannot be two opinions, but perhaps there may be no impropriety in confining our view of its meaning, to the careless and irreverent speeches into which, on trifling occasions, the name of the Lord is too often permitted to enter. We may here refrain from dwelling on the greater offence, as

## THE THIRD COMMANDMENT.

that is in fact comprehended in the ninth commandment, which will be the subject of another notice.

Taking "the name of the Lord in vain," is often done by youth, who having had examples before them, suppose using words which they had heard prohibited to children, is manly. So wretched an assertion of freedom will be likely, at no distant period, to bring sorrow in its train. The habit of using bad language once acquired, cannot be dismissed at pleasure, and it will often burst out where even the worldly interests of the speaker, would enjoin rigid abstinence from all expressions that can offend pious ears. To employ expletives weakens language, but the utterance of reprobate phrases deforms it. Far from giving to a youth a reputation for courage, good breeding, or wit, it marks him for a person of low habits, wanting in reflection and self-command. Infinitely more decorous, more dignified, is a chaste simplicity of speech.

> "In conversation be sincere,
> Keep conscience, as the noon-tide clear;
> Think how all-seeing God thy ways,
> Thy every secret thought surveys."

# THE FOURTH COMMANDMENT.

"Remember the Sabbath day to keep it holy. Six days shalt thou labour, and do all thy work: But the seventh day is the sabbath of the Lord thy God: in it thou shalt not do any work, thou, nor thy son, nor thy daughter, thy manservant, nor thy maidservant, nor thy cattle, nor thy stranger that is within thy gates: for in six days the Lord made heaven and earth, the sea, and all that in them is, and rested the seventh day: wherefore the Lord blessed the sabbath day and hallowed it."—EXODUS, chap. xx., verses 8—11.

---

IF in the decalogue, the Lord commanded the Jews to respect the Sabbath and to keep it holy, it was not the mandate of a king calling on his subjects to sing his praise, only to please his ear; it was a precious gift; a mighty benefit granted to the world of his creation. On that day, he enjoined his chosen people, and through them it is understood, all mankind, to do no manner of work. The repose thus willed to man, necessarily carries with it a season of rest for a large portion of the brute creation. Though as a simple rule of policy, the boon would be of immense value, and might wisely have been promulgated by a mortal ruler, no human authority could have given it such extensive influence, such all but universal observance, as the Holy Sabbath hath obtained.

From the commandment we learn that the

## THE FOURTH COMMANDMENT.

Sabbath is in fact a commemoration of the completion of God's great work—the creation of the world.

It has been mentioned as matter of inference, that the inferior animals share in the blessing vouchsafed by the Sabbatic institution. It ought to be known that they are especially included in it. In the fifth chapter of Deuteronomy Moses recapitulating the terms of God's covenant with the Israelites, not only exempts the manservant and maidservant from toil on that day, but distinctly adds, " nor thine ox, nor thine ass, nor any of thy cattle."

To the Christian, one other interesting reason for respecting the Sabbath will be suggested by the fact, that it was on the Sabbath after his crucifixion, that Jesus appeared to his disciples.

> " On the first Christian sabbath eve
>     When his disciples met,
> O'er his lost fellowship to grieve,
>     Nor knew the Scripture yet.
> Lo, in their midst his form was seen,
>     The form in which he died,
> Their master's marred and wounded mien,
>     His hands, his feet, his side.
> Then were they glad their Lord to know,
>     And worshipped, yet with fear,
> Jesus again thy presence show,
>     Meet thy disciples here."—*Montgomery*.

THE FIFTH COMMANDMENT

# THE FIFTH COMMANDMENT.

"Honour thy father and thy mother; that thy days may be long upon the land which the Lord thy God giveth thee."
—Exodus, chap. xx., verse 12.

---

The peace of society, and the happiness of the individuals composing it, largely depend on the careful observance of the fifth commandment.

It has been the pleasure of the Almighty to plant in the bosom of parents, that constant enduring affection for their offspring, which nothing can wholly subdue. Those who in the ordinary concerns of life, are found harsh and unsympathising, indifferent to the sorrows or the misfortunes of their fellow-creatures, turn to their children with tender anxiety, eager to save them from the slightest ill.

For a considerable portion of his non-age, the child is not only without the means of making any active return for the kindly care of which he is unceasingly the object, but he is even incapable of evincing gratitude. Clothing, food, and varieties of comforts are provided for him, at a great expense of toil and care, but he knows nothing, thinks nothing of the painful privations, to which his father and mother are

## THE FIFTH COMMANDMENT.

often subjected, that he may not know want. He in this resembles "children of a larger growth."

A well-disposed acute youth, whose mind is sufficiently enlarged to comprehend the anxiety and suffering which his father and mother have endured for years and years on his account, will feel it a pleasure, as well as a duty, to honour those who, while he was helpless and unconscious, fondly tended him.

The sacred volume, presents mournful instances of the dismal consequences which have visited the wicked disregard of the commandment. Every-day experience corroborates what we are there taught. Does a son rebel against his father, does a daughter neglect the affectionate admonitions of her mother, in either case, bitter reproach, shame, and poverty, are almost invariably seen to follow. It is, therefore, impossible too emphatically to impress on youth the fifth commandment as it is repeated, with some additions, by Moses in Deuteronomy—

"Honour thy father and thy mother, as the Lord thy God hath commanded thee; that thy days may be prolonged, and that it may go well with the in thee land which thee Lord thy God giveth thee."

THE SIXTH COMMANDMENT

# THE SIXTH COMMANDMENT.

"Thou shalt not kill."—Exodus, chap. xx., verse 13.

THERE is something so dreadful in the bare idea of murder, that little need be said to enforce the observance of the sixth commandment.

The first-born man, unhappily set an example of crime. Cain wickedly put his brother Abel to death. He has had many successors in guilt. Though the human mind naturally revolts at the thought of shedding a brother's blood, when the angry passions are called into play, when avarice has been disappointed, or pride wounded, the maddened gambler or the baffled suitor, has not scrupled to violate at once the laws of God and man, and incur the guilt of homicide.

How fearfully the crime of murder provokes the wrath of the Deity may be traced in numerous cases of modern date. Where human laws have failed to reach the assassin, and affluence and joy seemed to gladden his days, the death-bed confession has revealed the awful truth, that conscience avenged the fatal deed, and the agonies of remorse constituted a more exquisite, a more enduring punishment, than any minister of justice could inflict.

## THE SIXTH COMMANDMENT.

And wonderful have been the means by which the crime perpetrated in the stillness of midnight, and in a remote forest or obscure chamber, which no human eye could behold, has been brought to light. The very artifices, which the ingenuity of depraved men have adopted to prevent the deed being discovered, or to save themselves from suspicion and pursuit, an all-seeing Providence has used to bring them to justice. Not unfrequently has the culprit when about to ascend the scaffold, declared that with all the terrors of a painful and ignominious death before him, even in that sad moment, he experienced less anguish than he had felt from the gnawing worm—the self-accusing thought within, while danger appeared remote, and his crime remained unknown.

The murderer may escape human justice, but he cannot escape the searcher of all hearts; he cannot escape himself. His life is a chaos of shame and terror, and oh! at the last how different his end, from that of "those who have lived a virtuous life, to whom death is but the messenger who brings the tidings of life and liberty!"

THE SEVENTH COMMANDMENT

# THE SEVENTH COMMANDMENT.

"Thou shalt not commit adultery."—EXODUS, chap. xx., verse 4.

---

THE seventh commandment is directed against an offence, which has often proved fruitful of evil to thoughtless mortals, who have disdained to pay just attention to the precepts of divine wisdom.

We read in the Scripture, that when the Almighty had created human beings to inhabit this world, he blessed them and said, "be fruitful and multiply, and replenish the earth." Man and wife were ordained to be one flesh, so indissolubly one as to be inseparable, and in respect to them, issued the injunction, "what God hath joined together, let not man put asunder."

The prohibition of adultery, is in fact the prohibition of discord and bloodshed. To recount the strife, the murders, and the suicides to which it has led, would be an endless task. In all ages the condemnation pronounced against it, has been signal and severe; yet such the weakness and the wickedness of mankind, not a few of those who have been looked up to with general admiration for their talents and their worth, have in this respect been faulty;

## THE SEVENTH COMMANDMENT.

yet, as a writer of the last century has said, "all its evils cannot be reckoned,"—but the same author proceeds only to mention a few. It must introduce a total confusion as to the offspring, a defeating of rightful heirs, or utter obscurity as to family descents and pedigrees; for where this offence has found its way no man can know his own children, nor even ostensible brothers and sisters ascertain their relationship to each other; for which, as well as for many wise causes, doubtless it was (as well as to preserve the sanctity of the marriage institution) made capital by the divine law-giver. This we may humbly presume to be the case; for this offence is introductory of that kind of disorder, which must in the very nature of it, tend to destroy every bond of civil and religious society, and make the world in a moral sense a mere chaos.

The Jews punished those who broke this commandment by stoning them to death. Let the wise be warned in time to shun the danger, so shall a merciful Father—

> "From all temptations them defend
> And keep them stedfast to the end;
> Ever abiding in his love
> Until they join the church above."

THE EIGTH COMMANDMENT

# THE EIGHTH COMMANDMENT.

"Thou shalt not steal."—Exodus, chap. xx., verse 15.

---

The obvious importance of restraining covetous men, from seizing and converting to their own use what belongs to another, can hardly have escaped the most reckless. Let any one put to himself the thought how deeply he would feel aggrieved, if that for which he has been painfully toiling through months, perhaps through years, were snatched from him by a stranger, and then, he will understand how truly desirable it is that the eighth commandment should be constantly borne in mind, and strictly enforced.

Stealing we are not to understand, relates merely to the outrages committed by the housebreaker, the highwayman, or the pickpocket. The cheat who borrows from a confiding friend, without intending to return the loan, the plausible sharper who takes up goods for which he never intends to pay, and the capitalist who buys property at an awfully reduced price from those who by fraudulent means have obtained it from the rightful owners, all offend against the commandment "Thou shalt not steal."

## THE EIGHTH COMMANDMENT.

Yet in modern days, it is melancholy to know that many of these larger depredators, who by various artifices get into their possession that for which others laboured, have the effrontery to appear in the temples of religion, as if they were eager to be the instruments of divine mercy, to promote " peace on earth and goodwill to men:" they who by their heartless rapacity, have set brother against brother, and reduced whole families to despair.

Did reason prevail avarice would subside: did man reflect how brief the span of his existence, he would not so ardently strive for what it is not in the nature of things that he should long enjoy; it would whisper to him, " The proudest monuments of human art moulder into dust. Even the works of nature wax old and decay. In the midst of this universal tendency to change, could you expect that to your frame alone, a permanent duration would be given? All who have gone before you have submitted to the stroke of death. All who have to come after you, shall undergo the same fate. The great and the good, the prince and the peasant, the renowned and the obscure, travel alike the road which leads to the grave." Would not this thought check the unhallowed strivings of dishonest men?

THE NINTH COMMANDMENT.

# THE NINTH COMMANDMENT.

"Thou shalt not bear false witness against thy neighbour."—
EXODUS, chap. xx., verse 16.

FALSEHOOD leads to falsehood; the man who has unjustly made war on his neighbour, seeks to secure himself by a new sin against truth, and will frequently prevail on others to confirm what he has advanced: that is, to bear false witness.

This shocking crime strikes at the very existence of human society; it goes to destroy all confidence between man and man. He who would be respected here, who hopes for happiness hereafter, should sedulously cultivate a sacred regard for truth, and not lay upon his soul the withering consciousness of having offended against the ninth commandment.

In the Bible we meet with many cases, in which false witnesses have been signally detected and righteously punished. The annals of modern times, furnish evidence to the same effect. The depraved being who is willing to bear false witness against a neighbour, dreams not at the outset what a difficult task he undertakes to perform. To sustain, or effectually to disguise one falsehood, fifty more are likely

## THE NINTH COMMANDMENT.

to be found necessary; and all these to save their author from shame, must be in perfect harmony; like the parts of speech in a sentence, they must agree in case, number, and gender. One little error, and the whole fabric of fiction is overthrown, and the detected crime covers the false witness with undying shame.

If love of virtue, if admiration of the simple majesty of truth, failed to warm the heart, the prudent youth, studious not of duty to others, but of his own ease alone, would refrain from falsehood. The long, laborious, dangerous burden which it imposes, the indolent would shrink from; the talent and ever-watchful presence of mind requisite to guard against being found out, demand powers, which but few of the vain, are vain enough to suppose they possess. Beware then of bearing false witness, for the innocent are told, "Behold your God will come and save you; thus the eyes of the blind shall be opened, and the ears of the deaf shall be unstopped; and the tongue of the dumb shall sing."

THE TENTH COMMANDMENT

# THE TENTH COMMANDMENT.

"Thou shalt not covet thy neighbour's house, thou shalt not covet thy neighbour's wife, nor his manservant, nor his maidservant, nor his ox, nor his ass, nor any thing that is thy neighbour's."—Exodus, chap. xx., verse 17.

These words, says Moses, as we read in the fifth chapter of Deuteronomy, the Lord spoke unto all the assembled Israelites, "in the mount (Mount Sinai) out of the midst of the fire of the cloud and of the thick darkness, and he wrote them on two tables of stone." The scene was as magnificently awful, as the law then communicated was important and enduring. "And all the people saw the thunderings and the lightnings, and the noise of the trumpet, and the mountains smoking, and when the people saw it they removed and stood afar off."

Some little negligence an the part of the translator, speaks of objects being seen which are only made known to man by his sense of hearing, but who can deny that the circumstances here described, as attendant on the delivery of the law, combined those sights and sounds which are fittest to strike the mind with reverential awe, as at once appalling and sublime?

## THE TENTH COMMANDMENT.

The tenth commandment is a summary of some of the injunctions set forth singly in the preceding ones. It teaches that the true worshipper of God, will be a stranger to avarice. He will not envy a neighbour his wealth, or his happiness. He will not experience a desire to take to himself what another may rightfully claim.

With such clear and unequivocal condemnation of the lust of gain, it behoves those faithful ministers, who on each succeeding Sabbath, stand before the sons of men as the interpreters of the will of God, strongly to impress this great lesson on their hearers. They ought to do more; they ought to prove by their lives, that the golden toys, and the transient delights, which the thoughtless waste their days in seeking to secure and realise, have but moderate attractions for them; for the followers of Him who had not where to rest his head. Their thoughts fixed on things above, should render them superior to meanness and rapacity; taught as they have been that it is "easier for a camel to pass through the eye of a needle, than for a rich man to enter the kingdom of God."

www.ingramcontent.com/pod-product-compliance
Lightning Source LLC
Chambersburg PA
CBHW080327170426
43194CB00014B/2485